Marya...

Happiness is a choice
Beauty is not
Aren't you lucky!
You have both!

Dick Larson 05

Surviving
Ned Johnson!

A memoir by
Dick Larson

Dick Larson Books
Surviving Ned Johnson!
A memoir by Dick Larson

Dick Larson Books   © 2003 by Dick Larson
PO Box 11629   All Rights Reserved.
Naples, FL 34101   Printed in the USA.
dlarsonbooks@aol.com   1 2 3 4 5 6 7 8 9 10 Printing

ISBN 0-9740769-0-2
Library of Congress Control Number: 2003104569

DISCLAIMER

This book is written and intended to be a memoir of the years of association between Dick Larson and Ned Johnson. The information contained within is the facts, circumstances, and behaviors as recalled by Dick Larson. While many facts can be corroborated, it must be noted that this is a memoir and the retelling will to some extent be influenced by the author's perceptions and feelings at the time. Every effort has been made to provide complete and accurate information on this subject. Please send requests for additional information to the Publisher. If possible, such requests will be answered in future editions of this book.

The author and the Publisher shall have neither liability nor responsibility to any person or entity with respect to any loss or damage caused or alleged to be caused directly or indirectly by the information contained in this book.

Cover Design: Rik Feeney
Cover graphic: © Microsoft Clipart Gallery, picture # j0309599.

CONTENTS

<u>CONTENTS - continued</u>

FOREWORD

I don't know what you would call a book like this. An unauthorized biography, an unauthorized sketch or profile, a memoir, or maybe a long news article similar to some of the writings in the New Yorker. One thing is for sure. It's the truth, it's first hand, and it's been lived and is still going on. In the process of trying to remain friendly with Ned Johnson, the most powerful financial figure in the 20th century, I flew too close to the flame and burned up. I lost my friend, my money, my job, my lawsuit, but not my self-respect, because I'm dumb or naive, or both.

When one person controls $1,400,000,000,000.00 (1.4 trillion) and can do what he wants to do with it, he has a lot of sycophants buzzing around him, and he likes it. He knows they are in it for the money, not out of any love or respect for him, but he chooses to ignore that at this time.

He has one goal; a promise to his daughter Abby. A promise he made when she was ten and went in nights with him to check on operations. His promise; "Someday you'll run this whole company." That was 30 some years ago when it was questionable whether there would ever be a Fidelity, a small mutual fund at the time handling $3,000,000,000.00 and dropping. Now, it's growth, far beyond Ned's own vision, makes the old promise quaint, a nice gesture and dream for his beautiful little ten-year-old daughter, an outmoded idea he clings to.

Many of the key people at Fidelity are aware of the danger the company is in trying to live up to that old promise. In fact, employees are leaving because they're losing faith. Bob Posen, a key factor in controlling the fund managers, has left recently and not under the best of circumstances. He's teaching at Harvard and is on the team in Washington, DC trying to privatize the investing of social security money. Rumor has it that he and Abby Johnson didn't get along; good-bye, Bob. Four top managers have left this year (2002) to join American Express in Boston, which is in direct competition with Fidelity. There are many little wars going and Ned seems to be spending an inordinate amount of time putting out big and little fires.

My problems with the Chairman are minor to the financial world, but they may give the reader an insight into the future, if you can read between the lines and draw the proper conclusion.

***

As a reminder to myself that it takes many talents to create a book, I acknowledge the following people:

To the love of my life, my wife Sarah, for staying with me all of these years.

To Amy Dangler who never refused an assignment day or night to help this book progress.

To Rik Feeney, editor & marketing agent for all the help he's given me..., such talent, I am lucky to have met him.

CHAPTER 1 – NAHANT

It seems everyone we know talks about writing a book, and they probably should. Because some day in the future, maybe one or two hundred years from now, a distant relative will find it in the attic, read it, publish it and extend your lifetime. You have to be careful of the subject matter if you write about yourself. It becomes a simple chronology of you, your family and everyone else's family. We live similar lives, except for a few. This book is about one of the few.

Edward Crosby Johnson, the 3rd, is how he likes his name spelled. He likes to be called Ned by his friends and business associates. I used to call him Ned until two hours in August of 2000 split a friendship of 28 years. Now I have a number of different names not commonly used by those close to the great oracle. Let's establish, therefore, that this sometimes comedic, sometimes not funny at all book is not about Dick Larson. It's about Ned Johnson, however, since I lived every minute of it, I have to tell you something about my upbringing before wading into the private life of the subject. I promise to be short on the author and long on the favored one.

The favored one owns Fidelity Investments, the most powerful financial presence in the world today, and nobody really knows him. The Johnson's own 49% of the closely held, not publicly traded stock in FMR. Company. Top executives and fund managers hold the balance with the proviso if any of the above, except the Johnson's, wish to sell; they must sell to the family at a fair market rate. Who sets the rate? Who knows? In 2000, the year of contention, the company was handling 1.4 trillion dollars of other people's money (to be known as O.P.M. from herein) and was able to direct it to any investment they chose without the knowledge or consent of those who had bought that particular mutual fund Make no mistake about it, have no illusions, don't believe what you hear and only half of what you see, Ned privately owns and runs Fidelity without the checks and balances of a corporation, or board, or anything else. Everyone, including the family, is frightened by his sometimes irrational tirades. He has 1.4 trillion at his command. He can tank any stock market – maybe all. He can punish any publicly traded company. He is the most powerful financial man in the world, and when I mentioned this fact to him several years ago, his answer was, "Isn't that interesting!"

Ned talked with me frequently by phone in 1995 when we began construction of his house on Long Pond in Maine. It was not unusual for him to call three or four times a week during the two and half years we constructed. He loved it as I did. We thrashed out a lot of stuff, not all related to construction. I had been an English Literature major with a minor in history, and had carried those interests throughout life. I had worked as a plumber and built with my father a shop with 500 to 600 men by 1988. I had worked as a construction manager at Fidelity for five years and finished my career working directly for Ned for five and one-half years in Maine. I had developed enough business and social sophistication to keep him as a friend from 1972 to 1995, and a very close friend from 1995 to 2000. I believe he was my best friend for that six-year period.

E.C.J.3rd was brought up to trust no one. His father's admonishment was, "We have no friends, only interests." Also "What is in it for me?" Whether it was business or friendship, it had to be financially rewarding, or he would discard the deal, or the friend. I learned this the hard way. I should have known better. I was street smart early in life. I knew what a con artist and a wise guy were like and how to handle connivers. I didn't think he fit any of those characteristics; he fit them all. I was fooled. It cost me a small fortune. He ended up with everything he wanted. I went home to Florida with nothing. Ned was a great businessman, but a poor friend who couldn't be trusted. I had been told by several executives at Fidelity Properties, the construction and design division, known as "Ned's Playpen," that any promises he makes – get it in writing. I couldn't believe that of my friend. Much to my chagrin they proved to be right. So I've decided to put it in writing now.

***

In 1950, my third year at Tufts College, I quit, walked to the bursar's office, got my money back for the second semester of my Junior year, then walked to a small plumbing shop my father was running in Medford and applied for a job. I was experienced. I had worked summers for several years for them as a truck driver and helper. The shop was failing. I was broke and my father wasn't too well.

I had had enough. I needed a complete change. I needed to make some money and I needed to help my father out. In addition, I had met the love of my life, Sarah, at St. Stephens Church and I wanted to marry her. I got all four of my goals. I talked my father into going into business with me and started to make some money. I talked Sarah into marrying me six months later. I was so lucky at work and love, and a good poker player; my friends started calling me "Lucky."

Sarah and I had two sons and one daughter that we loved dearly. Sarah and the children provided the impetus for me to pump up the company from 1952 to 1967 into a strong position in mechanical contracting on the North

Shore of Boston with sixty or seventy good mechanics; a great business and moneymaker.

I sold my first house in Lynn, made a fair profit, and bought an acre of land for $20,000.00 in Nahant on the ocean facing northeast towards Salem and the sailing port of Marblehead and beyond to the fishing center of Gloucester. We built a two level house of sliding doors, glass from floor to ceiling, a three car garage on a circular driveway and a lovely swimming pool hanging out over the ledges that led to the waterfront; very rocky and scenic.

We spent twenty-three great years there raising three children, playing golf and tennis, on what was a virtual island with a narrow three-mile causeway out from the city of Lynn. The plumbing business was good. We worked at it, loved it, and soon had more work than we could handle. We developed some great accounts, built-up to six hundred men and managed, with the help of good assistants, to keep ahead of the surge of work and keep everybody happy.

We played tennis at two nice clubs, the Nahant Country Club with four clay courts, and the Carey Club with two composition courts, and a pool on the ocean. We were active in the management of the clubs as were our children. We met a lot of nice families, including the Johnson group and many influential people in the Boston business circles – lawyers, doctors and financial folks – and played a lot of tennis with everyone.

In the seventies and early eighties, we had formed a closer relationship with Lilly and Ned Johnson. Sarah, Ned and I playing with a partner, and Lilly, who didn't play, cheered us on. We attended parties at the Johnson's and had them over for dinner several times. We felt a nice friendship had developed and had great fun with them and many other couples from Nahant.

That's how the whole process began; how it all ended is in this book. One thing we were thankful for was keeping all our old friends and adding the new to the mix.

We still have our old school friends from the Highlands in Lynn, and I believe we're still thought well of in Nahant and at Fidelity Investments, except for one guy who happens to own the place.

Gulp.

CHAPTER 2 – TENNIS CHAMPS

In the early seventies, I called Ned to be my partner in a tennis tournament at the Nahant Country Club in town, a small seaside community twenty miles north of Boston with the population of 4,500 people. Sometimes severe storms swept in from the northeast. A three-mile causeway ran out to this town from Lynn, a shoemaking city since the Civil War. The causeway was cut and Nahant became an island for a few days. As you drove home from work on Friday nights during tennis, golf, and sailing seasons, the common goal was to mentally pull up the drawbridge until Monday, and have some fun and privacy with your friends over the weekend.

On this particular weekend in July, we were involved in a men's doubles championship match that was important to club members and but didn't mean squat to anyone else. Of course, we fought mightily for the trophy, and if we won, we were full of ourselves and obnoxious to the rest of the club for that season.

I had called Ned, because he was a strong defensive player, and he accepted. I told him to be on court four at 9:00 a.m. prepared to do battle or die.

"I will do just that," he said.

I said, "Fine, don't hit the wine, be ready at nine, the trophy will be thine and also mine."

"Geez," he said, "did you just make that up?"

"Never mind, just be on time."

And he was. He arrived with his racket that needed a new grip since his days at Harvard and was a bit moldy, one can of used tennis balls, dressed appropriately in a white shirt, white tennis shorts and unfortunately, underneath, long boxer shorts with blue and gray vertical stripes that hung out eight inches below his tennis pants.

He had to walk the length of courts one, two and three to court four, which he did with nonchalant aplomb. A ripple of laughter as he passed each court showed the true feelings of the men playing and the gathering spectators as they watched this apparition.

I greeted him, "Good morning, partner!"

"Good morning."

"You know our opponents," I said as I waved to them.

"Oh yes, hi guys!"

We began to warm-up and when I thought it appropriate I said, "Ned, that outfit is quite different."

"Yes."

"Did Lilly see you leave the house?"

"Yes, she didn't like the outfit."

"Oh, what seemed to be wrong?"

"She thought the underwear didn't match up."

"I see."

"I thought I would take some scissors and shorten them, but they are brand new. I didn't want to ruin them. They're one of three in a package."

"You're fine. Shall we start?"

"Yep."

To me, this was the beginning of a beautiful friendship. I loved any guy who thought that way; especially a guy who was on his way to becoming the most powerful financial man in the world. Nothing like the obvious and oblivious eccentric who hasn't got a clue, except in one narrowly focused area, his was finance.

We won our first match and were set up to play at 2:00 p.m. in the quarterfinals. He went home to lunch as did I and arrived back at the courts at 1:45 p.m. I had told Sarah, my wife, who did not watch the first round, that she would be missing something if she didn't come for the second. She did, but Ned showed up with his outfit slightly altered. Somebody had taken safety pins and curled up his boxer shorts to his tennis shorts by pinning twelve inches along the hem.

We began. Halfway through the first set his boxers began to droop in a scalloped fashion reminding me of the entrance to a tent during a joust. Well, we won. A good deal of laughing and joking may have helped our cause. At the end, the field of battle was strewn with safety pins, which after the match Ned dutifully picked up, with my help of course.

On Sunday we were to start at 9:00 a.m. in the semi's and were quite proud of ourselves and of the strategy we had planned after winning on Saturday. We had assessed our opponents' strengths and weaknesses (forgetting about our own, of course) and vowed to meet at 8:45 to vanquish those guys.

Saturday night Sarah had gone through my bureau and found a package of new jockey shorts. She suggested I call Ned and loan him the package for Sunday's match. I said I would call early in the morning and make the offer politically, because I swear he felt he was dressed just fine.

On Sunday I called at 8:00 a.m. Lilly answered, "Hello."

"Hi Lilly, it's Dick."

"Yes Dick, are you looking for Ned?"

"Yes."

"He's in Boston."

"In Boston?" I said, alarmed. "Lilly, we have a match at nine at the club."

"I know, he left early to get his underwear," she replied.

"Oh geez."

"Dick, he has plenty of underwear he just forgets it."

"Okay, let's hope he makes it."

"He will."

He did make it on time and was dressed to the nines; no clown this time. No win either. Our opponents were not distracted.

After the match, he and I went to my house to swim in the pool. He had filled his with sand so nobody would fall in, drown, and sue. We swam and Sarah served us some cold lemonade and cookies on the pool deck. Usually after a tennis match, the people whom we played with, or against, would come over to cool off and offer post-mortems on the tournament. Not this guy. He ate his cookies and drank his lemonade, and looked out to sea (we lived on the ocean) and said to me, "What are the duties of a financial partner on a large construction project?"

"To furnish the money," I answered.

"With interest?" he munched.

"Without interest."

"Why not?"

"Any bank will loan the money with interest without being a partner."

"Do they approve payments?" he munched.

"Not if you manage the project."

"Who signs off on requisitions?"

"Your project manager and your architects."

I felt like I was being grilled. Tennis was long gone. Business was the order of the day, serious business, and obviously on his mind since the weekend started.

When he left, I told Sarah I thought highly of him. I liked him. He was no phony. He was down to earth, but a dual personality. The question is, which one are you dealing with, the clown or the king?

CHAPTER 3 – BRIBING AND SMUGGLING

Lilly had decided in the late seventies Ned and a few members of the family needed a good trek. Nepal was the answer. Nothing else would do to change a few outlooks on life in Boston. Arrangements were made, time was put aside, training went into effect – mostly by the women – the men, in their forties, felt they were in good shape. They weren't as things turned out.

When they returned from Nepal an announcement was posted in the library and spread around the small town. Lilly and Ned were going to put on a slide show one evening at the picturesque Nahant Public Library. Sarah and I went to the show, which was put on mostly by Lilly with Ned standing aside for support that consisted of nodding his head in approval of each slide and discussion. He looked drawn, pale, and thin. Lilly was the picture of health.

I don't recall all of the slides, or comments, but I came out with several facts that remain in my memory. They flew to Katmandu, the capital of Nepal. The plan was to trek in to meet the culture gradually, rather than fly a chopper in and land in the lives of strange people with a thud.

The trek began with an uphill climb towards Everest, in which the men began to fall behind from day one. They were wishing, says Ned they had trained a little more. In fact, my understanding was as the group climbed, the men fell more than a day back. The Nepalese had furnished them with guides and porters without whom, Lilly commented, they could not have made the trek. There were icy rivers, fast flowing streams and crevasses, all of which required delicate crossings on rope slung bridges, or in some cases wading through shallows; strange feats for an inexperienced group of Boston Brahmins. Guides became indispensable until a few days passed giving the trekkers their mountain legs.

I believe they made their destination, the foothills of Everest, from which point having learned about the natives and their families, their religious symbols and way of life, the plan was to fly out on a small plane. I believe a DC-3 to the International Airport back in Katmandu and home. When the slide show was over we went up to thank them and Lilly said, "Ned, tell Dick and Sarah about what you had to do to get us out of the foothills."

"Well," says Ned, "we walked back to a small landing field, probably a two day hike. When we got there we had missed the plane for that day and there's only one plane per day. The eight of us secured lodging in a native hut with not much to eat and, as we sadly discovered, only one can of beer left. We ate native food that night. They offered some fermented milk as an evening cocktail. We declined. We slept chummy as on a small boat. In the morning, we packed and walked onto the small airstrip to board the plane when it came in. Much to our chagrin, the plane landed, the natives with baskets of vegetables and crates of chickens stepped in front of the door and they started to board. I went to the front of the plane and yelled up at the pilot. 'The Johnson group — we have a reservation.' He smiled, put his arm out the window, made a strange gesture and said something I couldn't understand. He closed the window. I ran to the door of the plane and spoke to what I thought was a porter, or loading guy. He looked at me with a grin as he closed the door and said 'tomorrow, tomorrow.' I related this to a groaning group. We trudged back to our hut for another night without good food, or cocktail hour. This whole business continued for five or six days. We were all getting comatose. Someone in the group finally said, 'What is this pilot trying to tell you Ned?'

'I don't know.'

'Does he rub his thumb and two fingers together?'

'Yes.'

'Jesus Christ, he wants a bribe.'

'What?' I said, 'I can't bribe anyone. I'm the President of Fidelity.'

'Not here you're not. You're just a gullible American. Jesus, give him some money and lets get the hell out of here.'

The plane lands. I run to the pilot's window. He holds out his hand and rubs. I yell and nod my head. He says, or rather gestures 'how many?' I say eight. He says forty dollars in Nepalese. I nod affirmatively. Out of the plane come chicken crates, vegetable baskets, and Nepalese. On goes the Johnson group, off goes the plane. I give the co-pilot forty dollars and we head to Katmandu. The folks who were with us on the trek were not happy with me. I will never forget the word 'bakseech' which means, 'give me some money and I will take care of you.'"

He ends the conversation by cautioning us never to tell anyone he's a briber. It might get back to the authorities in Katmandu, or Boston.

CHAPTER 4 – ALZHEIMER'S, FARMERS & CRASHING

In the Wall Street Journal a few years ago, a columnist posed a question "What did Ned Johnson eat for breakfast?" Financial types wanted to find something they could attribute his success to, how he made so much money, how he structured his companies, and how he maintained growth, astonishing growth. I now have the answer to the breakfast question: Three types of dry cereal with two or three types of fruit piled on accompanied by Chinese green tea boiled in his 240 volt kettle acquired in Europe (boiling time 20 seconds). The real question posed by his former classmates at Milton Academy and Harvard, who considered him a geek, was where did the talent come from and where was it when they knew him? Judge for yourself. Hiring the right people is part of the answer, but far from being the whole. Being lucky and patient? We'll see.

Ned Johnson, from what I have seen in thirty years, is a neurotic business savant who fell into a small business that worked well with his mentality and built it into the most powerful, privately owned, financial firm by a lot of luck, spelled Lynch. Peter Lynch built Fidelity. He made a fortune for Ned allowing him to play games with small ventures – some successful, some not. Peter Lynch arrived in 1972 to a floundering three-billion-dollar mutual fund firm started by E.C.J., 2nd, pitched in with a very small group of people, including Ned, and in eighteen years, laid the groundwork of the current $1,400,000,000,000.00 gross business. Lynch quit in 1990, burnt out from hands on, files on the floor and old-style sheer hard work. Ned commented to me in Maine he had not asked Lynch to work that hard, that many hours and almost kill himself. Lynch did it to himself said Ned. I detected some guilt feelings in his remarks. He summed up his role by saying he had nothing to do with Lynch's work ethics. Well, I commented, I was sure he hadn't driven Lynch; on the other hand he hadn't stopped him. "Why of course not," he'd answered incredulously. "Who would have?" Cash cows don't come into being in everyone's life. Today his thoughts on Lynch are not favorable particularly when we see him on the TV ads. Ned's unfailing comment to me is, "It's too bad he doesn't know what he's talking about."

People at Fidelity claim Ned's father started the mutual fund business and he may have. He was elected to Fortune Magazine's Hall of Business Fame as the second star. E.C.J., 2nd retired when Ned took over in 1972, the year Lynch came on board. The father retired star Jerry Tsai with a check for $18,000,000.00 and the comment that the only other candidate had the name Johnson, and that made the difference. Father Johnson was highly respected by most of his business associates. Comments like trustworthy, cool, apolitical, and fair are his legacy. He retired with early symptoms of Alzheimer's and died a few years later with what proved to be a severe case of the dreaded disease. I believe Ned has been haunted by this apparently inherited illness. His actions, diet and strange comments to me personally over the years have made me suspect that at 72, he's a frightened man, and I feel for him, it can be a 24-hour nightmare.

A case in point, in June of 1989, we were invited to the engagement party of Annie Garmey to be held at the Country Club in Brookline. We had just sold our home in Nahant where we had lived for 23 years. The Garmey's were our good neighbors; who had sold and moved to Boston several years before. We had all belonged to the same tennis and swim club, including the

Johnson's, and had socialized at the summer dances and the tennis matches.

Sarah and I had moved to a farm in Brookfield, New Hampshire, which had been left to us by the most unsociable couple, Ed and Iola White, you could ever meet. Ed White and I had built a soapbox derby cart in 1940 and won the Championship of B. Class in Lynn. The White's were very cranky. Whenever I mentioned we were going to drop-in on our way skiing, my kids groaned and moaned, and almost refused, including Sarah. I, on the other hand had liked them and got a hoot out of their unsociable behavior. I was and am, thick skinned – a product of my upbringing on the Highlands. Anyway, when our children had grown up and left, the White's had grown old and sickly. They had no children or relatives to take care of them, so Sarah and I pitched in for two years and when they died, God love them; they left us the farm. Sarah and I became farmers for five years.

We were pleased with Ron and Diana Garmey's invitation and looked forward to seeing our old friends from Nahant. We arrived at the appointed hour around seven in the evening. The party was underway with the babble that comes from an open bar. We made our way through the crowd slowly, meeting many from the old town and noting business luminaries, and legal eagles whom we didn't know, all lining up for a drink on our poor ex-neighbor. Poor Garmey.

Sarah and I were standing off to the side with other folks when Ned walked in with his family. He started looking around and spotted me standing at the far end of the room. Slowed by admirers, he headed our way and I said to Sarah, here comes Ned. He arrived in the midst of a busy area of the bar and in his best booming style, said to me, "Guess what?"

I said, "What?"

He said, "I've got Alzheimer's."

I replied, "You have not."

He said, "I have too. I've just been checked this week and I've got it."

I said, "Ned, do me a favor, come down here." We moved to a quiet corner near the kitchen door, Sarah moved off into the crowd. I said, "Ned you shouldn't announce something like that in a crowd like this."

He replied, "I don't give a damn."

"Not a good idea," I said.

"Well I've got it and I am looking for a couple of friends like you to help out."

I answered, "I'll do anything that's needed, but Christ nobody knows what to do anyway. What the hell can anybody do?"

"Well, I don't know. I've got to join Lilly and be sociable. I'll talk to you later. I will call."

From that night on until our friendship broke up in 2000. I treated him with great deference when he talked about his problem. I never again mentioned the word Alzheimer's, referred to his memory, his forgetting, or if his behavior was odd, I never pointed it out or blamed it in front of him to any form of mental illness, including dementia, anxiety or paranoia. All of which, I believe, he has. I was told I could have won at the trial had I brought up the above subjects, but my attorneys and I gave our word we would not, and we lived up to it. We lost.

In 1972, when Ned took over the company, it was small by today's standards – $3,000,000,000.00 under management. By 1973, it had dropped to $2,000,000,000.00. Ned was so disturbed he called a meeting of the few people who worked for the small company, including Peter Lynch. He made a simple speech. The gist of it being he had not taken over Fidelity to see it go down the drain. The solution was to start shooting craps, start gambling, take chances, stop being the stodgy old Boston Firm and if you lose, nobody will blame you, and you will have another chance, unless you do something stupid, then you will get fired with severance pay. The company took off like a rocket with Ned playing the part of the visionary oracle, meaning he stayed out of everybody's way as they built the company up to the point where it could afford such an oracle. That happened and it worked through the seventies and part way through the eighties, until the crash of 1987 when his crystal ball broke.

The oracle woke up one morning to a dropping market that prompted him to panic and push the thing into a near disaster according to some people at the SEC. The oracle got the finger from the First National Bank of Boston when he called during the day for a five hundred million dollar loan. He may have had by this time that much money of his own, but of course, the Johnson Law of O.P.M. ruled and he wasn't about to change that rule and risk his own funds. Someone suggested it looked like a melt down, but Ned sweeping aside and stepping through the redemption phone slips had an idea. If the banks don't care about the potential of a market crash and he didn't care about a crash (O.P.M.) maybe the US Government would care. Think of all those government employees out of work, who could ever be re-elected if this happened? Why the possibility existed those senators and congressmen might have to find a job and go to work like everyone else. Heavens to Betsy, something would have to be done. Well the great oracle came through and did the one thing he had been trained for and hopefully would never have to do again. He called the Treasurer of the United States and explained he couldn't cover the redemption demand. The Treasurer wanted to know why and where had all the money gone? Don't you understand, says Ned, it's fully invested in stocks and bonds and we can't sell them to get cash to avoid the crash, because everyone is scared to buy and we can't sell.

"What's the solution?" says the Treasurer.

The solution," says Ned, "is to call the bank, tell them to loan us the money (O.P.M.) and you guarantee the loan with the backing of the US Treasury (O.P.M.)."

And they did just that. The theory of O.P.M. surfaced again and proved to be a winner. Some say that to this day Ned caused the crash. The SEC pointed some fingers in his direction, but soon waffled. He's just too big a dog to pick a fight with. The market regained its composure within a year or so and so did Ned. And on to bigger and much better pickings as we make our way to the unofficial office of the great oracle, soon to be "King of the Market."

CHAPTER 5 – MUSSEL STEW

In 1989, I had closed my business and become a farmer in Brookfield, New Hampshire. We cut the lawn on two riding mowers, planted huge gardens on both sides of the house and renovated the kitchen, which was vintage 1902. The five cultivated acres were completed with growing gardens when we attended Annie's engagement party as previously written in June. In August, just before final picking season, we decided to take a three-day vacation and visit Lilly and Ned unannounced at their summer home on Mt. Desert Island. We had spent a good deal of time on the island at Bar Harbor and Acadia National Park when the children were young. The park had good hiking, great scenery, and the best lobsters in the world. We arrived on Friday late afternoon. Grabbed a small motel we had visited before, had a swim at 6:00 p.m., a cocktail at 7:00 p.m. and a big lobster at 7:30 in that order. After a good nights sleep in that cool Maine air, we got up early and went hiking along the Cadillac Mountain Ridge Trail. Simply the best on the East Coast and it's highest point as a coastal mountain. After a quiet afternoon resting and reading out by the pool, I called Ned at Long Pond in Somesville; he was there and invited us for a drink.

About six we drove over to what we assumed would be a nice house. Maybe even a lodge. What a surprise – the place was a dump! Ned was outside sitting in a rickety old chair on a raft with a ramp out to it – all of which had seen better days. Lilly was not there. He said she had gone somewhere to take a hot bath, which turned out to be the Causeway Club in Southwest Harbor. Things didn't feel right to us. They may have been fighting. We chatted with Ned for a few minutes, then Sarah started signaling we should move along. I began to prepare Ned for our quiet retreat when he noticed and insisted we wait for Lilly, have some wine and something to eat. At that point, Lilly drove up looking discombobulated and not too happy; when she saw Sarah and me, she perked up. He had not told her of the plans or that we had called. She seemed delighted. I think they were bored, and when we walked into the cottage, we could tell why. What a dull depressing shamble of an old place. Who wouldn't be unhappy in a place that was falling apart? Everything was leaning in one direction, including a rusted brown refrigerator, all the kitchen cabinets, the linoleum, the ceilings, the light fixtures and I particularly noticed the dishes, silverware, and Welch's Grape Jelly glasses circa 1950's. There was an old Essex tub with lion's feet; the toilet was heading south as was the lavatory (with one faucet) and as Lilly announced, no hot water. Ned seemed perfectly comfortable and composed just standing in what passed for a living room without a stick of furniture. We were in a state of disbelief at the dilapidated camp of one of the wealthiest couples in the world.

Lilly's enthusiasm somehow infected all of us as she outlined her plans for the evening. We also felt what's good enough for the Johnson's must be okay and therefore good enough for us. We talked or deluded ourselves into a firm belief the place was "quaint." First, we were to hike on Indian Point, which had been preserved by several families including the Johnson's to the tune of two million. Then, go home for a drink, supper, and then to bed after a swim in the pond. I could see the hike, I couldn't figure out where cocktails, dinner and sleeping quarters were going to come from, but who am I when miracles are conjured up by the Oracle. Anyway, we piled into Lilly's Volvo wagon in good spirits and went hiking at Indian Point. A great path along the water, seals, and Osprey nests and seaweed covered rocks, which Ned and I proceeded to walk out on in the spirit of adventure. And, at the furthest point, I picked up a huge flop of water-soaked seaweed, and low and behold there were hundreds of beautiful black, gleaming mussels just for the picking. Well, Ned, who is nothing if not a creative cook made round nests out of seaweed and we start picking. We filled the nests and every pocket we had. We were soaking in salt water, but much good would come of this he assured me. We made our way to the car, the girl's picking-up loose mussels as we dropped them. Ned knowing I had lost a lot of money that year in business, about $3,000,000.00, announced he would teach us how to live frugally in the future. He was going to make mussel stew for supper. I groaned inwardly. I wouldn't walk across the street for a free mussel dinner. Now I am about to be initiated on my vacation by a guy whom I know doesn't like over-cooked seafood. We stopped on the way back so Lilly could pick up a small pre-cooked chicken and a box of saltines. I could visualize the scrumptious repast we were about to have. Our contribution, unbeknownst to the Johnson's, was a basket of fresh tomatoes, string beans, onions, carrots, and potatoes from our garden. And, thanks be to the Lord, a great big beautiful bottle of Dewars scotch with which I hoped to drown my taste buds.

Ned went to work immediately with a pressure cooker resurrected from under one of the counter cabinets. The gasket, which had corroded, leaked and filled the small kitchen area with steam as he began the stew. He rummaged through our basket and selected things along with suspicious old bottles of things in the cabinet that looked to me like shellac and paint thinner from the past. Lilly and Sarah set the breakfast nook table, which was painted pale ivory and found in every house in America built from 1932 to 1950; all in the same color. I was designated bartender and dispensed that life saving liquid, and truly, man's best friend (not the Bernard), Dewars scotch. There was no ice, so we had to sip it straight. Ned's blonde head when seen was wreathed in swirling steam, but he was happy in his element – cooking up a lecture for his poor wayward friends and dinner. Lilly had decided to have the string beans and carrots as raw appetizers, because she doesn't like to cook. So we sat on the floor sipping scotch while Ned occasionally would peep out of the mist and toast the three of us with his jelly glass and jump back into the steam, reminding me of a stoker on an old coal fired British Battleship. Shortly the dreaded announcement – Ned exclaiming the stew was ready and must be eaten while hot. The table was set and we three sat down while Ned emerged from the fog with the stew. He poured an equal amount into each soup dish. Lilly lit the candle. Sarah gave us each one saltine. The chicken had been denuded of any meat. This specimen must have been the scrawniest fowl in the barnyard and we were ready to dig in, but first a lecture.

"Now," says Ned, "since you two have contributed all your assets to the Bank of New England, this is how you are going to live if you hope to survive." "The stew," says he, "cost twenty-seven cents a plate, the cracker is one cent, the chicken was on sale at $2.95 (beyond the purchase date obviously), so that's about seventy-four cents totaling about one dollar and two cents for each person. Let's eat." The stew, believe it or not, was terrific. He can cook with imagination as long as he doesn't drink too much before creating, which we were careful he didn't. I even enjoyed my cracker and Lilly gave me two small pieces of chicken, which I lingered over so as not to appear like I was pigging out. I didn't dare ask for another cracker in fear of upping the cost of each plate.

Ned got up during the meal, got four jelly glasses and a bottle of wine. He opened the wine, which he had wrapped in a towel like any good wine steward, and poured each a generous dollop. I thought that was nice of him. He put the wine on the floor, which I thought was odd of him and continued with his dinner. My first sip was delicious, as was my second. Everybody was tasting it without comment. I became suspicious. He wouldn't look at me. I asked him to tell me what it was, but he evaded the question. I reached down unwrapped the bottle and in the dimness of the candle I read "Vosne Romani Conti" 1981, a great wine for any table, a collectors wine and an expensive wine. I sat up straight and with a gleam in my eye said, "this won't do, this wine doesn't fit the budget you've outlined. Without looking, he slurped his stew and grumbled softly, "We don't want to carry this too far."

We didn't stay that night. We couldn't stand the thought of having anyone, including Lilly and Ned sleeping on the floor. We made our excuses. Lilly wanted us to stay and was making plans for the following day. We convinced her the farm and it's livestock needed attention, and we took off for the motel. The next day we drove home to Brookfield, the lawn, the garden and the cat.

We didn't see the Johnson's until the December wedding of Annie Garmey, which was held at Trinity church in Boston. The ceremony started about six-thirty in the evening. A full church and a snowy night made for a lovely interior scene at Trinity – a tribute to Annie and her family. She was well liked for her modest ways, as well as her beauty. The reception was to be at the Chilton Club, a short walk from the church through four or five inches of newly fallen snow, slanting into the streetlights and lit doorways of the brownstones of Boston. It was a nice addition to the ambiance of the night and what would prove to be a life changing conversation for Sarah and I. A short line had formed on the stairs leading up to the function rooms. Several of Ron Garmey's friends, knowing he could be a little tight with a dollar, joked Ron had set up the delay and would close down the open bar before we reached the top. Of course, this didn't happen, but Ned commented Ron was looking a little peaked and wondered what was wrong. I commented the color would return once people stopped drinking and started dancing, which proved to be the case.

Ned approached me during the evening and inquired about my work at the farm. I said we had a great season finishing all gardens and grounds in September, painted the barn and took-off cross-country to Custer's Last Stand in October – great trip seeing the Northern plains by the seat of our pants. "And now what?" he asked. "Boredom for the winter? Come to Boston and work for Fidelity. We have plenty to do. We have our own construction division called Fidelity Properties."

"Gee, I appreciate it Ned, but I'm not sure I could afford to move to Boston."

"Aw, come on, I will give you whatever you need to get started, a house, a car, cash, whatever."

"Well, I can't commit right now, I'd need housing, I can't run two houses on my retirement income."

"How about this, you come down on Monday and see Ed Finn. I will call him and set up your appointment; and another thing, you could be the Project Manager for the Salem Armory Project."

I thought for a moment and said, "You know something, I can drive to Salem in one and one-half hours. I wouldn't need a thing."

"There you are," said Ned, I'll set that up, you call Finn's office and make your appointment."

I spent the rest of the evening dancing, dining and extrapolating on my new career. Little did I know thirteen years later, I would have to fight for my financial life in a courtroom in Bangor, Maine.

CHAPTER 6 – THE INTERVIEW

On Monday, we were off to Boston for our introduction to Fidelity Investments and it's subsidiaries. It was exciting to think of trying something new, particularly with the sponsor I had. I felt empowered as anyone would with that kind of backing. The first person I met with was a human resources young lady who had a yellow file folder and a manual that looked important. I had never worked for anybody but myself and probably was as strange to the corporate culture as they were to me. I didn't know the meaning of the word politics, or pecking order, or fear of speaking out. I didn't know humor was out of place when speaking to a president or vice-president of a division. And so, we launched what turned out to be a disastrous interview. The young lady did not refer to her materials at all, but asked me two questions. "What position would you like?" and I responded kidding, "something high-up." "What would you like to be paid?" I responded, "One hundred thousand a year." She smiled and thought my answer was perfect and we moved on to meet the president of Properties, Ed Finn.

Now, unknown to me, Finn was not only an all-American football player at Brown, he had also become an astute corporate politician, a survivor. He survived by becoming Teflon coated. He wouldn't sign anything. He wouldn't be responsible for anything, he wouldn't initiate anything, nor would he put himself in the position of being or taking any blame for anything. The way you do this is you bring several friends from your previous employer and make them all Senior Vice-Presidents. In this case five, and indicate if any problems come to his office from their division that could possibly stain him, they would be fired, and lose the cushiest job they ever had. They would have to go out and work in the real world.

In we go to the great man's office, couches and leather chairs were set in a semi-circle away from his desk area, so as to make all of us feel we were on equal ground - democracy at work. We sat down; Finn started the conversation with a lukewarm greeting and welcome to Fidelity. I noticed an odd tic consisting of flapping his right cheek with his right hand, not too obtrusively at first. He commented Ned had called and indicated to him I might do well in the construction division. I replied I thought that would be the best place for me. Finn then asked what I would like to be, or do. I, trying to lighten things up said, "Why don't I be the President."

Finn turned and looked out the window at the old State House with a sigh tinged with sorrow. With the hand flop accelerating against his cheek, he turned back to face me with sagging lids and answered, "You can't be."

I said, "Why not?" and he said, "Because I am the president." "Oh," I replied. Things were quiet for a minute. The resources person smiled at me with what I thought was encouragement that things were going well, and he liked me and my humor. Then the great one turned away again, hand flapping and said, "What do you expect to receive for salary?"

I replied, encouraged by the young lady's demeanor, "Oh, I would say $150,000.00." A dead calm settled in the room. Silence broken only by the slap, slap of Finn's face by his own hand.

"Well," said Finn as he slowly swiveled in his chair. "I see you have done a good job of preparing Mr. Larson for the interview and I thank you both. I will give consideration to the thought you've presented and be in touch with you both soon."

I left elated with myself. I had gauged things correctly. Of course, my joke about being president was not to be seriously considered, but the salary issue looked good. I did hear several days later from Finn, and I was offered $50,000.00 to start, plus benefits, which I accepted. The human resource person was never heard from or seen again around the Fidelity premises, in America, Europe, or South East Asia.

Work began for me in Boston where I was given a few small projects to do while waiting for the Salem project to open up. In the meantime, Sarah ran the farm and I stayed with my parents in Lynn, taking the blue line subway to Seven Water Street. I could begin to see Salem was not moving too fast and my boss Bob Wells suggested I make plans to work in Boston for a while. This required I take Ned up on his offer of housing. I took the issue to my boss and he took it to Ed Finn, who would presumably take some action to complete the negotiation and discussion I had with Ned. Nothing happened. Bob Wells suggested I drop the issue since it had become hot with Finn and he didn't want to get involved. I called Ned and reminded him of his promise. He called Finn, and with alacrity and alarm, Finn got me an apartment at Pine Banks, a housing complex owned by Fidelity for executives to live in with their families while on temporary assignment. That solved my housing issue.

Sarah came down and we stayed there for a year and a half, then paid rent for my final three and one-half years with Fidelity. However, that ended any kind of a friendly relationship with Finn, but I didn't mean anything to him or his world anyway, or vice versa.

Finn retired several years later and was replaced by a guy from the outside who was eventually nick-named "Skippy." We had a young, but mature and serious group of men in our division, about twelve who took their work seriously and performed under Bob Wells as a well-oiled machine. Bob was a damned good executive, a workaholic who should have been president of properties.

Instead, the first morning after the weekend Finn retired, I came down the street, cold and old with my gray fedora, scarf, heavy coat, and galoshes. I looked up at Finn's former office and in the window the new guy had put a metronome meaning time marches on. I was now a grizzled-old veteran project manager of three years – able to handle the Mothership Building at 82 Devonshire. In fact, I was now called the Duke of Devonshire by my colleagues on any project – a joke. The guy put a freaking timer in the God damned window. I pulled my coat collar up, crossed the icy street, spit on the old snow bank, and entered Seven Water Street. What did we have, I thought, a God damned Boy Scout? Well, little did he know the bell was tolling for him. He came and went, didn't bother anyone and we didn't bother him. He was harmless and soon placed in another spot in Fidelity where he couldn't cause any damage.

CHAPTER 7 – THE JOB

Having been hired in January 1990, and told to report to work on the second, my wife made me buy two new suits to go with the three I had, along with a pair of Johnston and Murphy shoes at two hundred-fifty dollars a pop (I cringed).

I settled in to a small office with the now dreaded cube walls and attached desks with a view of Washington Street. On my desk was a map of Boston, showing the buildings Fidelity rented or owned, including the World Trade Center complex, and a company phone book.

I was introduced to our secretary, the other twelve guys, the men's room and the elevator. When I returned to my office, my boss had laid ten job order forms from different groups requesting small construction projects.

I was totally lost. I went out and looked for the buildings on my map. I couldn't even find them. I returned to the office feeling somewhat inadequate with a little panic thrown in. I studied the forms for some clue. I noted at the bottom of each form was a contact person with a phone number. I called and connected with Rose Eppard. She suggested I meet with her that afternoon at two.

We met, talked and Rose said "Are you new?"
"Yes."
"First job at Fidelity?"
"Yes."
"Do you know what to do?"
"No."
"Do you want to know?"
"Yes."

"Over at your building, Seven Water Street, you have eight floors of experts. Fidelity is a very wealthy company and only hires experts, except in your case. Go back, go to the eighth floor, and have the manager assign an architect. You are on the seventh floor, therefore, you are the project manager. On the sixth floor have the manager assign a furniture person and a move coordinator, the fifth floor is contracts, the fourth is wiring and cable, the third is real estate and the second is the executive group under Ed Finn, so just skip that one."

"This is helpful Rose."

"Yes."

"I put the team together?"

"Yes."

"And the budget?"

"Yes."

"Then I put out bid documents as per the eighth floor?"

"Yes."

"Then what?"

Put them all together, including the contractor, in the conference room. Assign a tight schedule and start screaming."

"I don't scream well."

"You will."

"And if I don't'?"

"Buy some Valium."

After a few months, maybe four, I began to develop my own system of operations with our people, the outside architects, and contractors. Like any company, you soon identified those you could rely on and those who faked it.

We all had plenty to do. At one point, Fidelity was renewing 40% of its space nationally. That meant after two-and-one-half-years, you were demolishing jobs you felt you had just finished. Incredible growth and what, to us in construction, was appalling waste. However, when you're handling billions of dollars daily, you couldn't fool around with salvage or re-use. The word was just get it done. Put the people making the money back in bigger and better quarters with more complex sophisticated equipment and let them go.

I frequently lunched at a small restaurant near Quaker Lane. Several years later, as I walked through, I noticed a big green round construction chute from the sixth floor. Down come all my new mahogany doors with the special brass hardware attached. I thought, *my gosh there goes my first job for Rose Eppard into the dumpster.*

After two years of operations in the Boston area and other parts of the country, most of my assignments were at the Mothership building at 82 Devonshire Street.

I came in one morning and my boss had left a single order form that almost cost me my job. The assignment was Roof Top Garden, Fifth Floor, 82 Devonshire Street. It should have read: Hot Potato ala Ned Johnson, since that was his floor.

In the chairman's lobby were a series of small windows looking out on a tarred roof surrounded by high buildings on all four sides. Twelve large plastic pots filled with flowers represented the chairman's garden, hardly a scenic delight for the Captain's of American Industry to view as they visited Fidelity.

The assignment was to meet with the chairman, after selecting three finalists for the garden design, have the designers make their presentations to the chairman and let him select one design. The executives at Seven Water Street deemed this politically astute.

We began a search for garden designers. Lilly Johnson called me one day and alerted me to a lecture later in the week at night in the Boston Public Library that might be worthwhile, and as usual, she was right.

One in-house designer and I attended the lecture on Gardens of the World. A coffee table book by Julie

Meservey was on the counter as we entered and there standing at the podium was Julie herself – a tall, sophisticated, slender woman of beauty and graceful manner.

We were impressed with her presentation, so much that when she finished, we stepped down the carpeted stairs to the stage where she was gathering her materials and preparing to leave. We introduced ourselves. We spoke briefly about the project and whether or not she would be interested in the design competition. She was very much interested and we arranged to meet with her to visit and discuss the design parameters of the job along with the other two competitors. The program was to have them come up with sketches, which we would pay them for, and present them to us simply for discussion before presenting them to the chairman.

The preliminary presentations were made and accepted by our group for presentation to Ned. The appointment was set for a Thursday night starting at seven o'clock. We met at the fifth floor lobby; all of us nervous and feeling the pressure. I had an inkling the Meservey team had the inside track and decided to have her make the final presentation. After all, Lilly had thought enough of Julie to call me to attend her lecture.

Things went well with the first two presentations, with lots of questions, answers, and spirited discussion on both sides. When the second group left, I went out to the lobby and brought Julie in with her presentation. Ned was speechless. He was so taken with her we all started laughing, including Julie. A little embarrassed, she colored up to just the right skin tones.

The ball game was over. Julie set up a tripod easel, put a huge colored drawing of an oriental garden with a fourteen foot high bamboo fence for a background, islands of moss and growth to a sea of Mount Airey white gravel with an island in the middle and a focal tree that would change every month with the seasons.

We thought it was great. Ned had recovered somewhat from his surprise at our new star, enough to display his personality for her benefit. He thought he had been transported to the sensual gardens of Babylon or something. I think if any one of us had complained about anything she presented, we would have been reassigned to the Chelsea gas tanks.

Julie completed. Ned stood up and thanked her properly. She looked at me for relief, comic relief I guess. She was taken aback at her reception and her departure with him helping with the easel and door. Almost too much for her and me, and we started laughing aloud. He, of course, smiling and bowing didn't notice a thing.

Ned came back into the conference room after a while sat down and said to his assistant, "Well Charlie, what are your thoughts?"

Charlie says, "I thought they were all great."

Ned turned to me "Well Dick?"

"I think Julie is outstanding."

"Well" says Ned "I think Dick's right. She's head and shoulders above the rest."

Yes, I thought to myself, *you're making a Freudian slip. She's more than head and shoulders; she's the complete package.*

I left at nine-thirty with a verbal agreement for Julie. I rode the elevator down to the Devonshire Street exit and went into a bar that was next to our building. I had a scotch, then hopped the subway to Melrose and arrived home to Sarah. Mission accomplished so far.

The budget was complete and I was instructed to make an appointment with Ned, explain the items that made up the report and get his approval. We met at his office at a pre-arranged time. I waited in a small lobby leading into his personal secretary's office for about twenty minutes. Even though we had been friends for years in Nahant, I was on his turf and impressed with the atmosphere of reverence exhibited by those who worked closely with him on a day-to-day basis. Frankly, I started to get nervous.

Finally, the door opened and I was asked into a large room with three young ladies all smiling and busy at tasks I assumed one of the world's best businessmen had given to them. A young assistant opened his office door and I walked in to the "sanctum sanctorum" of E.C. Johnson, 3rd. There at the end of this richly adorned office sitting on a huge couch like a Buddha, with the largest pear shaped bowl of fresh strawberries and a small bowl of sugar, was the grinning Ned, my tennis partner and friend. I relaxed.

He got up, we shook hands, and as usual, he tried to out grip me. He squeezed my hand to make me give in. I didn't, so he tried to throw me to the ground. Finally, I gave in and started to run out kidding. He laughed triumphantly and indicated the violence was over and I should sit. This scene was nothing new. It happened every time we met at play or at work. He didn't care. He loved the expression of comradeship and wanted others to see how strong he was, and he was.

He looked the budget over and commented, "Will this do it?"

"I think so."

"I think you're too tight."

"I'm trying to be."

"Why?" he asked.

"Because I want to induce you into doing the job."

"You're going to get in trouble."

"Well" I answered, "It's $300,000.00, where do you go from there?"

"Add $50,000.00." he said.

"All right."

"I'll sign for the $350,000.00."

"Okay."

"If you go over, Finn will get rid of you."

"That doesn't bother me."

"Why not?" he asked.

"Because the gardens for you, and if I need more money to please you, they'll give it to me."

"Like hell," he said.

"We'll see," I replied.

It was a Mexican standoff.

I selected Payton Construction to do the project. I told Bill Payton how hot this was going to be politically because of its location, client, cost, and above all it had to be temple quality all the way. Every client who came to see the chairman, or his executives on some of the world's most serious business would see the garden as representing Fidelity's commitment to excellence and appreciation of their clients' business.

I told Payton I wanted to select the foreman for the job, responsible to me for all reporting of anything. He was to be dedicated twenty-four hours a day if need be. He was to put a trailer on the roof of 82 Devonshire ten floors up he could use as an office or sleeping quarters. My wish would be his command with no negative response, just do it. There was only one job super for me, a young man, best of all, a skinny young man who smoked. His name was Jim Thonis and without him over the next several years, I would not have succeeded in some of my toughest jobs.

Jim Thonis added years to my life as a project manager at Fidelity. Projects in Boston are tough anyway, but if you have an accident, you take a big hit stress wise, because of the consequences. Not only for the people involved, but also the company and the city, and it's old infrastructure. A particularly difficult task is cutting into water, sewer, or gas mains in the middle of a busy street. This causes stress on everyone involved in any major city in the country.

Jim and I got into a hell of a job before the garden that had to be done at night, off hours in the middle of Congress Street just over the hill heading south from

Quincy Market. We had to cut a valve into a City of Boston water main. This was a no-slip-up piece of work and dangerous to boot.

We organized for a week almost to the point of rehearsal. We hired two of Boston's finest, we had on orange hard hats, orange and black sawhorse barriers, lights, rubber orange barrels, backhoes and the materials needed times two since supply houses are not open at midnight.

On the appointed night, we had everything ready, including several key men from the city water department. I hung around until seven-thirty. Jim said go home, piece of cake. I told him to call when it's done. He says no, get a good night's sleep. You're too old for this stuff. He was right. I went home and called him on his portable phone at eleven o'clock just as he had gotten started. He reported they had set-up and were underway and indicated all was fine.

The next morning I arrived early at my office. Jim was waiting in the lobby when I came in. I acted nonchalant and asked him if we were all set. He replied the job was complete, but they'd had a little problem.

I sat down in my office and Jim sat down, and started a narrative of the event. My boss Bob Wells came in to listen. He was a little nervous too. "Well" says Jim, "here's what took place. At eleven, we set up our barriers, lights, barrels, and cones. We moved one backhoe up stream to block any nut that couldn't see the rest of the stuff. We dug a 14' trench eight feet deep three feet wide and the guys jumped in to prepare the tap. Over the hill comes a guy doing about sixty. The officer at that end steps out to flag him down, since the speed limit there is thirty-five. The guy tries to avoid the upstream backhoe, skids and hits the first barrier plank, which hits the policeman and knocks him into the back of the trench."

By this time, Bob and I are horrified. Jim goes on, "We scrambled to get out of his way. He skids and rips off the rear tire by hitting the trench. He isn't going any further, so we put all our efforts into helping the injured officer. Within minutes we have police, firemen, an ambulance, and one helluva traffic jam."

"We placed the officer in the ambulance and sent him off. We put our men in the street and cleaned the mess and debris, so traffic could resume. After we cleaned-up, we finished the work at 4:00 a.m. and took a breather. We got a report from two officers in a cruiser on the guy driving the car. He was in serious trouble. First, he was driving a Porsche; second, he's from California; he was drunk; and lastly, he was a convert to Judaism. The cop, by the way, was okay and at home recovering."

Bob Wells looked at me and said, "He'll never get a fair trial in Boston."

I said, "They'll make another tea party in the harbor with cement blocks."

Jim said, "Actually, he wasn't a bad guy."

Bob said, "If only he had converted to Catholicism."

Jim Thonis finished with, "If he was Irish, he shoulda stayed that way."

Amen.

CHAPTER 8 – DUE DILIGENCE IN CHICAGO

I certainly was not the best project manager in our group of twelve. These young men with degrees in engineering from the fine schools around Boston, would run circles around me on computers and highly technical jobs. However, I did know construction old and new from my years as a contractor and I knew how to handle clients, craftsman, and their craftiness.

Judith Webster worked at Properties in the Real Estate Division. She had gotten involved in a building in Chicago owned by a commodity trader at the Chicago Exchange. This type of person bet his net worth every day, he must have been a walking ulcer. He needed a partner to renovate this 1890's fourteen-story building; he needed ten million from us.

The architect and I flew out several days ahead of Judith to start our inspection program. Our reservations were made at the Swiss Hotel. We were each given our own room at $500.00 a pop nightly. Fidelity is a class act. My room was big enough to hold ten people in comfort. In fact, it was bigger than some of the apartments my family of five lived in comfortably while growing up during World War II.

After breakfast the next day, we headed by cab down to the project in the middle of the city. It was indeed a lovely old building in the middle of everything. We went in and found the project manager. We chatted a bit. He thought since the elevators weren't in service, we might take the construction lift attached to the outside of the building for hoisting, ride up to the roof and walk down the stairwells floor by floor instead of climbing them.

We went down the alley to the staging lift, met a gruff old Irish guy who ran the thing and boarded for the ride up.

"Where to?" he asked.

"The roof." I said.

He put his pipe in his jaw, threw some gears and we were off rattling our way to the top. My partner and I watched the lead inserts that had been drilled into the brick to hold the elevator. They were all loose pushing and pulling out as we rolled by. I looked at him; he at me, we both rolled our eyes.

We reached the roof. The old guy slid the wire door open and gestured towards a plank fourteen inches wide and eight feet across to the roof.

"What are we supposed to do?" I asked.

"Walk onto the roof." he said.

"Listen, the ride up is bad enough," I answered "and we were stupid enough to have done it, but I'm not walking fourteen stories high on a fourteen inch plank."

"Ha, scared huh?" he replied.

"Listen you old bastard, you take us down, and you bring up a carpenter and three more planks and build a proper method to get on this roof."

He started laughing. We all started laughing. He started down and grinned at me, tobacco stained teeth. I said, "You son of a bitch." The more I cursed the more he laughed. We got what we wanted. Two hours later we started up again. All I had to do was stare at him and he'd laugh uncontrollably.

"Want me to pick you up at 5:00 p.m.? That's when we go home."

"You can go home at 4:00 p.m. as far as I'm concerned," I said. "We'll walk down. I wouldn't ride with you again. In fact, don't even come near me."

His head disappeared beneath the roof. All we heard was cackles of laughter and the rattling elevator. We completed our work in two days. Judith flew in on Thursday night for the meeting with the trades and the owner's rep on Friday at 10:00 am. That night we had dined together at the hotel. We gave her as much information as she could absorb. She then took the paperwork up to her room for study.

The next morning we took a cab and arrived just on time. We entered a large room that the construction people had cobbled together with about twelve chairs. It was time for Judith to strut her stuff. She opened the meeting by thanking everyone for coming to help us in determining if we wanted to invest.

"And now," she said, "I will turn the meeting over to Dick Larson for the remainder of the session." I was sitting there like "Dinny the Dunce" until her somewhat startling announcement. I recovered. I knew just about what we wanted to find out. I knew the type of tradesmen I was dealing with, so once I got going, we all did fine finishing up at noon time.

When done, we said our thanks and good-byes, walked out to a passing cab, and started for the airport. I looked at Judith who was not looking at me and said, "Young lady would you mind telling me what happened back there?"

"Guess what happened?," she said.

"What?"

"I took all your notes with me last night, lay down to read them, and fell asleep. I didn't know shit from shinola."

Later in the month I heard her report was excellent, however, we did not invest based on Judith's calculation, but it was a nice trip.

CHAPTER 9 – THE GARDEN OF PERIL

With a signed budget, we started planning the rooftop garden. Julie, who we found out later, had designed and been instrumental in the installation of the Azalea path at the Arnold Arboretum, was as good as we could ever have hoped for, and energetically pursued her tasks to get us off on the right foot.

I took various ideas to the chairman. He suggested it would be nice if Julie could meet with him instead of me, because he could answer her questions and save me for other things. I thought that would be nice and made a wise crack about her being better looking than me too. He responded it was just good business common sense *and* had nothing to do with looks. I, of course, didn't agree in a professional manner.

Jim Thonis and I met the next day, climbed out on the roof and started to dream up some ideas regarding the space we had to work with. We were measuring with tapes, a laser on a tripod for shooting grades, a ladder, and several masonry hammers for testing the bricks above and below the windows. None of the tools, and certainly neither Jimmy or I, were particularly interesting to construction peephole lookers, but a problem soon became apparent. We had an audience of seven or eight people loitering to see what we were going to do. This went on for several hours with the group changing guard every twenty minutes or so.

One of our most curious and faithful peepers throughout the construction was Jim Curvey. He managed to see through every type of sight barrier we erected, including brown craft paper, sheet rock, foam spray and last, but not least, some folding doors we had erected from dumpsters out in Quaker Lane. He went on to second in command and operating committee in the late nineties. He did a fine job for Fidelity.

As usual, Jim Thonis and I made decisions we felt would improve the job. The roof was too small. We decided to stage it five stories in a light well and add some steel to increase the area by fifty percent. This gave Julie a better palette to paint her picture. We were lucky too. Finding above the small windows heavy steel lintels installed when the builders built the building in the early nineteen hundreds. God love them.

We hoisted steel, toothed out brick, installed big picture windows, built concrete walls, installed flat roof drains, and kept our daily audience enthralled with jack hammers operated by strong arm handsome construction men in yellow hard hats. Our crew performed for the lovely young secretaries of Fidelity and romance blossomed after hours. One girl told me the bricklayers were the best. They would take them to the sleaziest bars in the market area for cheap drinks and she smiled as she thought of it. "We felt so safe being with them. They were gentlemen and saw to our transport safely home, or whatever." The "whatever" was left up in the air.

Julie had hired an engineering group to design the watering and filter systems, which would be automatic. The lighting she did on her own, along with the bamboo fence (from Taiwan), the moss and plants, the North Carolina white gravel, 150 bamboo trees, last the focal tree, which became an integral part (and remains so) of the garden. The focal tree was on Pork Chop Island that Julie had placed on the right hand section, the widest part of the space.

The focal tree is changed for each month of the year with seasonal connotations. In the fall, we have leaves lying on the island and the small mountains of green moss that run to the sea (gravel). In winter, the focal trees are changed bi-weekly, snow is on the ground. Christmas lights are on the fir tree in December, and of course the spring and summer seasons are appropriately recognized throughout the garden.

We spent a week setting the final plantings. Jim Curvey was the only one who broke through the secrecy of the installation. He had found, on one of the floors above, a viewing point that he kept secret. We managed to fool him by installing the island and focal tree during the final night, just a few minutes before Ned and Lilly being the first to see the completed garden. Curvey was home awaiting the Johnson's for dinner at seven. They got there at nine-thirty.

Lilly and Ned came out. She had four champagne glasses. He had a bottle of Moet-Chandon. Jimmy pulled the craft paper off in one swoop. Ned popped the champagne, which missed a sprinkler head by a fraction (so help me) and we all toasted the view of Fidelity's Rooftop Garden. The Johnson's had not seen it. They played fair like kids that wait for their presents on Christmas morning. They loved it, looking at it from every angle. Julie explained each plant as they listened intently. Ned challenged her use of the 150 bamboo trees saying they wouldn't survive in the New England climate; especially a zone seven, which is what Boston is to horticulturists. Julie responded they had tested the roof and with all the heat emanating from the surrounding buildings, it had tested out to a zone five. Ned was impressed with the thorough study she had made, along with being impressed with her, period.

The Johnson's left for the Curvey dinner party. It was about nine-thirty. Julie and I took the elevator down with them. The last thing the Johnson's saw from their limo was the two of us walking with arms around each other down Devonshire. We were exhausted and relieved. Julie gave me a kiss good-bye as we parted for our different subway stations. A small bar next to the Orange Line stairs beckoned to me with neon lights. I stepped in, ordered a Chivas on the rocks, and as I sipped my drink I looked in the bar mirror and toasted myself, and thought not bad old boy, not bad. I have never had a more pleasant ride home on the tube until the day I retired.

It would be nice to write everything lived (plants) happily ever after, however such was not the case. The plants started to die and the bamboo trees developed a form of lice that were eating the roots. The place smelled like a swamp, which, it turns out, was exactly what it had become.

Julie, Jim, and I held a meeting in the garden. Jim had a spade shovel and dug deeply into a section of the gravel. It came up soggy. The filter fabric laid in first was not allowing drainage. We were aghast. Everything would have to be taken out, the filter system had to be redesigned, and the garden planting re-done.

Here is where and why I got along so good with Jim Thonis. Nothing licked him. He could solve any problem if it was solvable. He said, you get the engineering done and I'll change this bastard over a weekend. That is exactly what he did. One month after the disaster, we scheduled the changeover for a Friday night start and worked twenty-four hours for two days. Jim finished it late Sunday, called me at home, and defied me to discover if anything had taken place that weekend. I looked on Monday morning and he was right. He was the best. The guy pulled me out of a political disaster.

Several years later, Ned and I were hiking up in Maine and he remarked the garden was still his pride and joy. I responded it came out well. We had a good team. He thought the operation had gone flawlessly, except he said, they had a little drainage problem, but they had fixed it with ease and it has not occurred again.

One month later, the Boston Newspapers came out with an article critical of the Chairman for spending

$350,000.00 on a garden, while having just told the fund managers there would be no bonus money for them, because of such a poor performance year. I was immediately called on the carpet for letting the budget out to the reporters. I had done no such thing, but my head started to roll off my shoulders as the senior staff on the second floor decided the easiest way to defend this was to blame the project manager.

As my employment became more uncertain, my boss Bob Wells stepped up to the plate and went with me to the staff meeting that had been called to deal with it. Ned was wild and about to fire someone.

Bob stood up and said, "This number the paper has reported is correct to the penny. I don't think Dick knows to the penny what the job cost is, it hasn't been finalized or sent to us."

"Who do you think released this?" said Finn.

"Oh" said Bob, "since these figures go through cost controls, accounting and disbursements, probably stroked by ten or twelve people; most of them young. Some of them party after work and maybe sit next to a reporter at the bars on newspaper row. Dick and I go home every night on the subway. We don't see or talk to anybody. Anybody who had the figures would be inclined to want to impress their companions with a story about a garden that cost $350,000.00 and that's how it got out."

The senior staff accepted that as a good defense, which it was. Ned was told and agreed stating, "It's something we have to live with. It's worth every penny to impress our clients."

Was the garden headache over? No, it was not. We hadn't dispensed with the lice that continued to eat the roots of our bamboo trees. We called Julie for the answer. She called the bamboo guys, wherever the hell they were. She called me back and said two words, "lady bugs." We found out where to order ladybugs and ordered 3,000 sent by Air Express (20 for each tree).

The lice were eaten and when they were gone, the ladybugs left for better hunting grounds in Boston. One of the Boston papers noted the yearly infestation of ladybugs. They stated they had arrived early, proving the theory of global warming, which would soon inundate the Coast Line of America. In the long run I guess, the garden would become an instrument of terror larger and more distractive than the big dig and for a lot less money.

Boston would have to be moved out to Worcester because of the early ladybugs. Don't blame Jim and me, we just followed orders.

CHAPTER 10 -THE INJUSTICE COLLECTOR

It's raining at 82 Devonshire Street. Ned needs a cab. There aren't any and its seven o'clock at night, probably 1987. He has to go somewhere fast and he's pissed off. He takes this stuff personally. He's an "Injustice Collector" ergo "Boston Coach" springs into life a few months later under the auspices of the "Prince of Darkness," James Curvey himself.

For fourteen years, the prince urged the fledgling company on through the streets of Boston and then on to other major cities. They made their first profit of $5,000,000.00 in 1999. They continued to expand. The last I heard they had replaced Chryslers with 8000 new black Volvos. Ned no longer waits, plus he is a constant back-seat driver (once grabbed the truck wheel out of my hands in Maine), and even while talking on the phone, he indulges himself with advice to the chauffeur.

The Boston Globe fell into the clutches of the injustice collector. Several years ago, after some bad press, the Prince of Darkness was assigned the task of buying all the community newspapers around Boston, about 125 of them and slowly strangling the poor Globe. Fidelity pulled their ads from the paper and the New York Times (which owns the Globe). The pen is still mightier than the sword and (I hope) the dollar. The fourth estate remains the average guy's best hope of surviving the financial onslaught of the big boys, which has increased in intensity since a few dolts (meaning us) made a few bucks in the market and were soon to return most of it.

The Prince sold out the newspaper business to the Globe's rival in Boston, the Herald. Steve Bailey the financial columnist for the Globe took umbrage in a recent column hinting Fidelity gave the Herald a big break, (injustice resolved, competition enhanced).

Someone talked Ned into starting a financial magazine in New York under the cognomen of "Worth," words dear to his heart. The Prince was assigned as the head of Fidelity Capital, better known in inner circles as other peoples money (O.P.M.), to shepherd this venture to the top of the literary heap. It never got there. It sold several years ago at a rumored loss of $50,000,000.00 of O.P.M.

While I worked at Fidelity from 1990 to 1995, a major decision was pending on the purchase of a new phone system called Vantage 20/20. I recall Ned struggling with that one. Some poor soul talked him into going forth boldly into the new century several years ahead. It didn't work out so hot and was junked several years later at a loss of $320,000,000.00.

Other kinds of collecting can be hard on the pocket book too. While traveling through China with head curator Tara Cedarholm, they spotted a 400-year-old Chinese house with two levels, balconies, and a bell tower. Ned immediately thought of the Peabody Museum project in Salem, Massachusetts.

One problem, there was no access or road into the treasure, so he had one built measuring one and one-half miles to the site. This began a series of events that continue to this day ten years later. The house had to be disassembled brick by brick, joist by joist inclusive of every item that goes into a Chinese house. Numbered, loaded into trucks, and carried to the embarkation point, where a friend, who owns cargo containers, picked it up and shipped it to a huge empty factory in Melrose, Massachusetts.

With the house came eight Chinese carpenters, one interpreter, one American project manager, a bunch of curators from Fidelity, and several restoration architects from New York. The goal after two years was to re-assemble the house inside the factory. This was done at a painfully slow pace, a private *pork* barrel for the help.

Upon completion, the question arose amongst the Architects about whether or not the house should be restored or displayed as is at the museum. A New York restoration firm was called in to help make the decision. It was decided to restore the building, unfortunately the restoration firm couldn't come to the site, the building had to be taken down piece by piece and shipped to their shop, not surprisingly. This was done to the best of my knowledge and then after restoration it was shipped back to Melrose and re-built. Ned had asked me to look in on occasion when I was in an apartment at the Melrose complex. I didn't know until the court case in 2002 I was considered a spy. My counter spy was the Chinese interpreter; she followed me so close. I swore she was coming on. I think had I gone to the men's room, she would have followed – but enough. I got bored and frustrated with this project, which cost about $30,000,000.00, to date.

The curatorial staff travels the real world and the Internet, bidding on a daily basis on a number of art pieces, Ned said about five. Thirty thousand people have offices or cubes, and each is entitled to at least one art piece, usually hung on the wall. There is a code; workers get one, small senior V.P.'s get two, large senior V.P.'s get three, and Ned gets four (Abby might get four). All this adds up to 35,000 pieces of corporate art. Ned's collection of art and furniture in the ten houses he uses worldwide is worth far more than all the corporate art combined.

The house in Maine has three Chippendales, one Hepplewhite, wonderful old Chinese pieces, valuable rugs, and paintings – conservatively a collection of $4,000,000.00 to $5,000,000.00. It's fun being around this stuff, forget the value, the quality seeps into your brain. You know it's a reward for relentless effort in the financial world. Does he know what he has? Yes. He is one of the world's most knowledgeable men about Chinese, Japanese and early American furniture, and the work that went into them. The picnic boat is named "Zitan" after a valuable oriental tree or wood.

American Express recently stole four of Ned's top executives and opened up shop in Boston. It happens all the time to all companies and can create bad karma amongst them. Imagine what happens when you unwittingly do this to an injustice collector.

When you hire young men and women with good credentials, degrees from the best schools, MBA's from the same, and you train them for five or six years until they're thirty or so and making several million a year you're going to have troubles. These people are close to primadonna status and are attractive to the outside world.

In steps an outfit like American Express and offers them the world. You have an option, pay the price or they walk. Ned doesn't pay. They walk. They need to be replaced, but with whom? Why, new young people of course; then, they have to step up as fund managers, for example, and perform immediately. That's one reason you have twenty-something-year-olds handling your mutual funds and retirement programs. Most of them don't have the experience.

A case in point; Peter Lynch retired as Magellan Fund Manager. He'd been great, but barely keeping up with the S and P in the end. He got his bonus of fifty three million and went home on the Blue Line subway to Wonderland, (that's not sarcasm, Wonderland is a gray hound track in Revere) the last stop. (On the other hand, betting tracks are not that far removed from the stock market).

Looking around for a replacement, Ned and Gary Burkhead spotted a rising young star in the person of Jeffrey Vinick, a nice young man who rode on the Orange Line subway. Jeff was young; it's true, but seemed talented. He was made Magellan Fund Manager with assets of over $70,000,000,000.00 at the time.

Things went well for a year until Jeff decided that although leading the pack, there might be better wind to port, so he leaves the group and started buying bonds. He had to prove his talent as the skipper who sees through the fog best of all.

The wind died, the bonds didn't produce, and Jeff fell behind. He shouldn't have tacked while ahead, he needed to go. Ned described the fateful day as attending a funeral in the morning and a wedding with Bob Stansky, a veteran skipper, in the afternoon. Magellan has never recovered momentum. At this date, May 18, 2002, it's down 12%.

To tie the loop, the injustice collector ordered all Fidelity people to tear up their Amex cards and all business in stocks and bonds of any kind was to cease forever. Meanwhile, be assured, someone has been assigned to investigate the possibility of severe punishment to AMEX. Fidelity owns 73 million shares of AMEX. (*Whoops...to be continued.*)

Recently, I had a meeting planned with Ned regarding some construction in Maine. When I arrived at his office, he came rushing out and said, "Come with me." We hustled down Devonshire. Me in good warm Maine clothes, he in a light unbuttoned raincoat, tie flying, suit coat flying, and no hat. "Where," I asked, "are we going?"

"To the new chart room."

"Why? I'm not very well dressed."

"You're fine. This is just a bunch of bullshit."

We arrived on the upper floor of one of the company's rental units and standing in a half circle are 50 of Fidelity's best fund managers. Gloom pervades. The market hasn't been doing well nor have they. The chart board has a bunch of up and down blips. Ned points to one up blip and says to the group "see that?"

"Yes," they all say.

"That just paid for our three new towers on the waterfront."

Everyone grins, but not too happily.

"Well, what's happening here?" he says.

Someone pipes up from the back, "It's not good."

"Oh, it'll come back," says Ned.

No answer, all gloom.

"Well," he says, "what shall we do?"

"Buy back the bonds."

"Whose bonds?"

"Vinik's bonds," said a brave soul.

"Like Hell, that would be a publicity disaster," says Ned.

We all file out. Ned needs something to eat. He always eats during disaster. We go back to his office. He calls the kitchen and orders food. Lilly had told me in Maine he always reacts this way to problems. We go through to the small private dining room and have small portions of picturesque something followed by lovely looking something's for dessert, all followed by pure green tea with leaves floating in the cup. I swear I weighed less than when I started. If I owned my own kitchen with three great chefs, I'd have Martinis and Filet Mignon every night.

I went back to Maine with my small problems leaving him with his big ones and dyspepsia. He'd call at odd times. I think to relieve his mind of the troubles of the world. He'd be on his way home at seven at night, call me with questions and direct the driver at the same time.

He'd be in the hot tub, or the shower and call, and I'd hear the water dripping. Thinking he was in Japan with Geisha attending to his needs, but no, just at Charles River Square. He had questions and answers, but I think he just wanted to talk to somebody who wasn't looking for something. He hadn't met many who weren't looking for money or help, or power-sharing and I believe he was tired of it.

He called one night at Christmas time and asked about bonus money for the workers. I suggested cash and he agreed. "Would $500.00 do for each carpenter?"

"You can't do that," I said. "You'd destroy the economy up here. Bob Bond, their boss is probably giving them $200.00, you can't undercut him."

"Jesus, you're right, you've been around."

"Yes, and if those guys got that much money, they'd quit for a month."

"Oh my gosh! We wouldn't get anything done," he said.

CHAPTER 11 – SHH..., I'VE GOT A SECRET!

He called late one night in 1998. "Dick."

"Yes."

"We've got a problem up there."

"Okay."

I was sitting on the side of the bed. It was winter. We always turned the heat down. Sarah got a blanket and my slippers. I looked at the clock and it was one o'clock in the morning.

"I want to talk about expenses up there."

"Okay."

"The electric bill came in at $137.00 for the month."

"Okay."

"The diesel fuel for the generator came in at $68.00."

"Okay."

"The lumber bill had some tools charged to us by the carpenter. What the hell are we doing buying his tools?"

"Hold up a minute. You have a fine caretaker hired by me and trained by you. Why are you calling your project manager?"

"I know, I know, but I can't get through to his mind. He doesn't have a clue. I have to talk to you." He knew he could jaw bone me and not hurt my feelings.

"Okay."

"Somebody is using the truck."

"Okay."

"They are using it too much and I want you to check it out."

"Okay."

"Now is there anything else I need to address. I am on my way to a meeting, I've got three guys here waiting for me."

"All right, ah, wait a minute, what do you mean a meeting? It's one o'clock in the morning. Where are you?"

"Taiwan." He hung up. I sat on the side of the bed. The call must have cost $2,000.00. What was the point? Why, of course. He was indirectly lecturing those three guys who were going to manage the Asian Markets fund on how to run a tight ship and how close he watches expenses. And, we think the Chinese are tricky.

We were together in Maine on Mt. Desert Island in late 1996, the home of Bar Harbor, Acadia National Park and many of the country's rich and famous from the Rockefellers, Fords, Johnson's, and Martha Stewart.

It was winter and we were in our new truck with four-wheel drive cruising down on Pretty Marsh Road towards Edward's new house. Being regular guys, we were talking in imitative "down Maine" slang and getting good at it. I was driving when Ned started looking under the seats, in the storage compartments, under the sun visors and under the dashboard.

"Did you lose something?" I asked.

"No."

"Well, what the hell are you looking for?"

"Microphones."

"Ned, this is our truck. There are no microphones in here."

"Just checking, just checking that's all."

"Geez, don't you trust me?"

"Yes, yes, but you never know. I have to be careful."

"Why?"

"I'm going to tell you something that is illegal and I could go to jail for it."

"Well," I said, "don't tell me."

"No, I want to. It's for your own good."

"Oh yeah?" I said.

The information was that I should buy COLT when it's issued, because he, with two other guys, owns it and it's going somewhere. What was it? "City of London Telecom" and it would open on the NASDAQ at 17 dollars per share. Hold it for one year or so, and get out. In my opinion, that information was illegal - insider information of the first water, right from the horse's mouth. I was in a state of shock. He could go to jail for it and so could I.

"Usually," I said, "These I.P.O.S. open a little high don't they?"

"Yep."

"Maybe I'd be better off to wait and see if it dips to 14 or so as often happens."

"That's up to you," said Ned.

"Would you do me a favor and let me know when it drops and perhaps I'll buy some?"

"I will," said Ned.

I never heard from him regarding the stock. Had I invested and had he been caught, I believe I would have had to testify against him and forfeit any gains.

I was in a quandary not of my own making. I didn't buy, or participate in any way. I didn't ask for any information because I didn't believe in his stock pickings. I had been involved in some of his requests regarding political donations to guys in the state of Massachusetts who weren't Irish, therefore unelectable, and anything he thought I should buy in Japan, which has been a ten year loser.

A few months later, we were on our way to play tennis, driving down Sergeants Drive beside Somme's

Sound when I said, "Hey, you never called me on COLT."

"Oh Jesus," he said, "Oh my God!"

"What? What?"

"It's gone way up."

"Up to what?"

"Oh, I think 530 from 17, I forgot to call you." said Ned.

He didn't forget. He gave me a once in a lifetime chance of becoming a multi-millionaire. I had $100,000.00. If I had invested in COLT it would have gone to $3,700,000.00. My mistake, my lack of faith in his judgment, his knowing I didn't trust his judgment prompted him to punish me by not calling. In the long run I'm probably lucky because if this comes out, he could be in and I could also."

It's his word against mine if it got to court, but someone else in Maine was given the same information and he bought. He invested $10,000.00 and shortly thereafter, he had $370,000.00 in the bank. How come a guy living in a remote town in Maine, doing some business with Ned, ends up buying a volatile stock in a company in London. Probably the only guy in the state who did so. The answer is obvious.

Ned had invested $33,000,000.00 with two young guys in London giving him majority control in the new public offering. With all of the splits, splats and maneuvers they ended up with $2,000,000,000.00 in the bank and probably all of his original investment back in his pocket. The stock has sunk to $2.08 per share as of April 2002. Oh, how the mighty have fallen, or have they? I don't know how the average investor made out, but I bet I know who did.

CHAPTER 12 – POLITICS

I must touch lightly on the politics at Fidelity. Like all large companies "politics" or "networking," such as "you wash my back I'll wash yours" exists. At Fidelity, it not only exists, it's a thriving business that erupts on occasion into outright verbal warfare. My personal friendship with Ned didn't go down well with certain executives in my division. My interview with Ed Finn, although humorous to me, wasn't taken that way by Finn. I had an air of independence and confidence that came out because I had worked for myself all my life; it was natural.

Failure on any project was tantamount to a ticket out the door, especially if the job either didn't work when completed or didn't finish on time. All of which cost Fidelity millions of dollars in trading hourly and cost you your job.

I was given the job of moving the library archives from one building on Devonshire to an adjacent building with space that had become available. I reviewed the space with a selected architect and an expert on libraries from Cleveland (all experts come from far away).

The project turned out well. We had to reinforce the floors with steel beams, which proved tricky because the floor below was occupied. The space was totally furnished, cabled and wired for the next several years, or until new systems were invented.

We planned to disconnect on a Friday night putting the library out of business until Sunday night, at which point, working all weekend, we'd move personal papers that would be boxed by the people who need them, plus we would connect everything up, turn on the systems and lights, and open the doors at 8:00 a.m. on Monday. Nobody would miss an hour of work, nor would Ned lose a nickel of income. Not to denigrate the job or the people who constructed the area, it took four months and was a reasonably difficult process.

We arrived on the Friday night of the big move. Our move coordinator and I met at the site. The disconnect was underway, the contractor and his outside subs were lined up and our Fidelity specialist was in place. The move would be a piece of cake on Saturday.

"Do you foresee any problems?" I asked.

"I don't," she answered. "I have your number in New Hampshire."

"Fine, call me if you have any problems, but call me on Sunday to report we're set."

I left with a 95 percent feeling things would go well. Always that five percent nag I'm not going to be there, however, I was only two hours away in case.

At 9:00 a.m. on Saturday morning, the phone rang: "Hello, Dick?"

"Yes?"

"This is Barbara," the coordinator.

"Yes Barbara."

"We have a major problem down here. The union electricians have gone on strike and have shut down the job. Nobody can work."

"Oh yeah?"

"Yes."

"Who's the foreman who called the strike?"

"It's Charley."

"Put him on."

Charley worked for Rotman Electric. Rotman had been working on our buildings since 1972. They knew all the systems and Charley had worked for that company on our jobs for 14 years.

"Hi Dick, it's Charley."

"Hi Charley. What's the problem?"

"Well, your people are coming in and hooking up phones, and connecting the furniture panel plugs."

I said, "It's an inter-company phone system and we have always connected the panels from your pre-wiring."

He replied, "I know, but I don't like it, so I've shut the job down."

I remained as calm as I could, while my mind was racing ahead. I had to do something drastic and I had to take a chance. Use some powerful language, not sure I had the power, and would have to gamble I'd be backed up.

"Charlie, I'll tell you what's going to happen."

"Okay," he said.

"How long have you been working for Fidelity?"

"I've been here working for Rotman about 14 years. You know I work for Rotman, not you."

"Let me remind you of something. Did you know down at the union hall there are a lot of guys. There's hardly any room on the benches because so many men are not working?"

"Yep."

"And when you run out of work you go back to the hall and I think the rule is you have to go to the end of the bench."

"Yeah, you do."

"Well Charley, that is exactly where you're going. You're going back to the union hall to the end of the bench, and Rotman Electric has done his last job for Fidelity."

He paused to think and asked, "Do you have that kind of power?"

I said, "Yes I do, and I will use it immediately. I will have Mass Electric in there by 1:00 p.m. to finish and you will never work for us again, nor will Rotman."

I could hear him sigh, then pause, and then he said, "Forget what's happened, the strike is off. We'll finish today. Sorry about that."

I said, "Have Barbara call me tonight. Thank you and good-bye."

She called, job complete, no more problems. "I don't know how you did it. You're a character." she said.

"If Charlie's there, tell him to come to my office at 8:00 a.m. Monday." Let him sweat the weekend.

Someone higher up was playing politics with my career. I was determined to find out whom.

CHAPTER 13 – RETIREMENT TO MAINE

While working early one morning in 1993 on the fourth floor of 82 Devonshire in the trust project the elevator stopped and out stepped Ned and Gary Burkhead, who at that time was running the fund managers. They poked around. I was doing a punch list and didn't pay a lot of attention to them. As they finished their tour and headed for the elevator Ned turned and said, "Don't be such a pusher." I was puzzled by the comment.

"Be patient, wait and see." Burkhead smiled. "Good things will happen to you."

I wasn't looking for anything. I was happy with my work and so was my boss. Later I thought they might promote me or something, or pay me more, or whatever. I wasn't overwhelmed with the comments, thank God, because I spent two years working from that point ending my career under whelmed. Nothing happened to me.

I retired and had a good party on the tenth floor of Twenty Seven State Street. My family showed up. Lilly and Ned, my friends, fellow workers and I had a pretty good roasting. Ned sidled up during the evening and said:

"Do one more year."

I said, "I couldn't do one more hour."

"Why not?"

"Because I'm 65 and too old to work in Boston."

"Well I'm 65 too."

"Yes, but you own Boston."

He laughed. We parted supposedly forever, still friends.

In April, I got a call from him. He had mentioned to me that he wanted to build a larger home on Mt. Desert Island, during the previous summer tennis season. I was happily golfing, biking and swimming, as all good retirees should do, but I lied. After four months, I wanted some action.

"Here's the deal: one house, one million, one year, no expenses except food, stay in the newly renovated guest cottage, what do you think?"

I said, "I like it. Sounds Great. What's the pay?"

"What do you think?"

"How about ten percent?"

"No, no, that's too much. How about seven percent?"

"I don't think I want to break up down here for a year for that amount."

"How about this," he said, "you do it for seven percent and if it comes out really good, I'll consider a bonus."

"Ned, lets do it for eight percent."

There was a long pause – "I'll tell you what," says Ned, "I won't agree to eight percent, but I'll pay it."

I laughed to myself thinking what in the world kind of deal is that. Let me tell you, he knew exactly what he was doing and I didn't have a clue. Seven years later, a judge and jury didn't have a clue either, but agreed with him much to my chagrin.

In June, we had lunch in Boston in the private dining room and discussed the details of the house as he saw it and wanted it. The plans were sketchy, not much to them, but at least a footprint to get me started. I went to his birthday party in Nahant on the 29th of June, collected the keys to the guest cottage and made an appointment to meet the following week in Maine.

On Sunday, little Dickie Larson and little Sarah Larson got in their little car and headed for the island. Had I been more alert to the danger of dealing with this cunning bear, I would have avoided the whole trap and turned south for Naples, Florida. He must have laughed at my naiveté and immaturity, my enthusiasm to work and produce good things, and not play games and politics. He's probably still amused at the simple minded couple. I forgot as I had been warned to get things in writing. He's forgotten, however, she and I both came from the Highlands in Lynn.

We arrived late Sunday, unpacked, and had a swim and a good night's sleep in the new cottage. The next morning dressed in a pair of shorts, tee shirt and sneakers, I took the plans and walked up the hill to the site of the new house. I had been told the foundation hole had been blasted out, which it had, but unfortunately, it was full of water and in the wrong place. I only had three sheets of plans. The rest were in a garage on the property. I looked, found nothing, and walked back out to the edge of the big rocky hole.

It was almost too much. I stood there feeling totally inadequate. The plans were incomplete, but as I studied what I had I realized the house could be doubled in size by raising the foundation, and with the decks that would have to go on or you'd fall out all the sliding doors, the house could more than triple.

What saved me from giving up and calling Ned was I knew I could build anything with time, and even more so, I had the money behind me. I went back down to the cottage for more coffee. Sarah had done her housework and was checking the loft. The sun was shimmering off the blue water lake. What the hell, so we'll have to stay longer. I didn't tell her that then.

We were off on the wrong foot. I'd had enough business and construction experience to know we had to stop. Put a stop to this immediately, go back, and start over correctly. I called Bill McHenry the architect, and asked him to meet that day with me. Bill came that afternoon. I said, "look, we've got to jump start this job by starting over."

He agreed.

I said, "We need a full set of plans and specifications. We need them to use as biddable documents, select five bidders and get them out."

He agreed and from that point until the end, five and a half years later, he and his assistant Brian Reading were the best. We made a damn good team without the intervention that kills many projects – ego.

In the meantime, while plans were being formulated, I poked around town for an excavation contractor and was lucky to meet Richard (Tater for his belly) Gray of Blanchard and Gray.

Tater came in the following week with heavy equipment, including the ledge blaster. When Ned heard this, he decided to come up and play. This was the beginning of a series of visits over the next three years I think were the best times he had had away from work. He loved the way Tater worked, and so did I. We had gotten lucky.

He loved to come up. He started to assume the persona of a "regular guy." A regular guy has definite qualities, which he and I defined over a period of time. He clothed himself in a checkered half coat of red and black with matching hat. He wore dark corduroy pants and pale yellow work shoes with a heavy tread and in the winter, overalls.

Regular guys knew their way around, on the job and in the woods, and rarely ever visited, or were seen in civilized places. They didn't look right. They knew their way around and could handle pick-up trucks, beer, construction equipment, rifles, shotguns, women, fish, boats, moose and deer including skinning, down Maine talk and humor, children, church and eating. They did not read books, hike for no reason, exercise, go home to pee, take a day off, watch television, swim unless drowning, or listen to advice from anyone.

Ned's idea of fun was to climb into the truck, me driving, and travel the scenic roads of Mt. Desert Island. Acting like a real guy, looking at their neighborhoods, houses, kids and stuff, taking delight in commenting on everything in his new found "Maine twang dialect."

I'd say something like, "the other side of the track."

"No, no," he'd chastise me, "those people live right, simple, non-stress and happy productive years. He was almost wistful about it. I frankly knew he couldn't have lasted, he needed, as did I, action. He'd say to me, "Let's go down this road ahead on the right, there might be something interesting to see." Down we'd go and sure enough here comes a nice home in a lovely setting and we would stop.

His first comments were complimentary, but I knew with further study he would express some derogatory remarks like, "See, the problem is the front steps and the chimney." I usually sat and waited. He'd continue, "They don't have a clue and it spoils the color when you look at the roof shingles, and the shutters are on backwards, see?" I nodded, "But it's not too bad other than those few details."

I'd say, "Well they're happy there and having a good time."

"Oh yes," and we'd move on.

The next house, which I thought was quite nice, turned out to be a total disaster. Worse than not having a clue, these people should be put in jail. "Why?" I asked.

"Because they set the house looking to the north. The whole house should have been turned to face the south. What a disaster." I sat there feeling bad for those people. Then it dawned on me, the cottage had a small sign over the front door that read, "Circa 1745."

"Hey, I pointed out to my friend that house was built in 1745. These people are not to blame."

"Well" he replied, "Someone back then is to blame. They should have shot him with a musket or stabbed him with a pitchfork."

We were all living together at the new guest cottage; Abby and Julia and her new daughter and granddaughter to Ned and Lilly. It was a Saturday night in August of 1996. Everyone had plans for the evening. All going our separate ways when we remembered Julia needed a baby-sitter. The best person I could think of was Wayne Merchant's wife Sally, who had mentioned earlier in the season that if we needed help she was available.

I called her and she agreed to come over and cover until Abby or her parents came back. Everyone dressed to get ready to leave at 6:45 p.m. for our dates. Ned started a strange project just as we were going out the door. He had become convinced, or obsessed with the railing leading to the loft. He, I think, was concerned Julia would climb the stairs and fall through. She couldn't even walk at this time. Abby asked him to stop. They were late. He wouldn't stop, or listen to her. He was in a trance it seemed and just kept working with heavy twine to weave safety into the railings.

Abby pretended to leave. Sarah and I stood mute, dumbfounded frankly by his stubbornness or intense focus to the point where he heard nothing.

Abby came back and demanded in strident tones that he come out immediately. He finished as she stood there, looked around as if lost and then walked out the door; a strange interlude to witness.

We waited for Sally and left for our date when she arrived. The next day I met Ned on the job and he mentioned what a lovely person Sally was (she works at the Town Hall full-time) and how pleased the family was to meet her. I said I had thought she could be called in on emergency, but she was a mother with a family and maybe best to find someone who didn't have the responsibilities Sally had.

"Well," said Ned, "I know she was a volunteer, but I slipped thirty-five dollars into her raincoat pocket."

"I wish you hadn't. They're very proud up here and like to do for neighbors and friends."

Several days later I saw Sally at Town Hall, thanked her for helping out, and mentioned Mr. Johnson had put something in her raincoat pocket while she was not looking.

"Oh Dick, that's not needed."

"I know, but you better check it out before you have it dry cleaned, or something."

That night I got a call from Sally. "Hi Dick, its Sally Merchant."

"Yes, Sally."

"Just for your information I did look in all my raincoat pockets and didn't find a thing."

"Gee, that's strange," I replied.

"It doesn't matter," she said, "I didn't want anything. I enjoyed the job."

"Well, thanks again," I said.

"Bye."

I hung up, sat, and thought, about how Edward and I were the tip checkers for Ned. I don't think he put a thing in her pocket to this day. It should have told me more than I learned from the entire evening. There is a saying about old people, who are not all there, not knowing "right from wrong," or the "consequences of their actions." He must have known I would hear from Sally either way, however, he was out to look good in front of his family, Sarah and I, and he didn't give a thought to the consequences.

CHAPTER 14 – THE CRITIC TURNS TO DOWSING

Our growing expertise in architecture took us all over the island. One day Ned called and told me he had an invitation from David Rockefeller, Jr. to view his new home in Seal Harbor.

We were in the middle of our main house project and trying to get some ideas, but mainly a handle on good craftsmen. He wanted to see the workmanship on the stone and brickwork, particularly the fireplace built by a company called Freshwater Stone in Orland, Maine.

"Do you want me to go too?"

"Of course, of course. What the hell do you think I'm calling you for?" he replied.

"I don't know. I don't want to butt in."

"For Christ's sake you're the project manager, you're my alter ego, you've got to go. What the hell are you thinking of?"

"Okay, okay, don't get your dander up."

"Pick me up in the truck," he said pleasantly.

"Okay."

"Great, Rockefeller's property manager will be there (it was winter time) and he is taking us through."

So, I picked him up several hours later and we headed off to David Jr.'s house. Ned had a habit when he was going through houses, and we were going through quite a few of them, of being a bit critical and the longer he was there the level of criticism increased. He would begin to compare their house to the one we were building in a reasonably loud unfavorable manner.

I would caution him when we were heading to our destination and while we were there in a low voice, I told him (and he needed this mild chastisement in many ways) he had to be careful about his comments, and at this house, the maintenance man would be with us. He might hear one of your comments and report to David, Jr.

"The smart looking guy had some bad comments on the house, Mr. Rockefeller."

"Oh really?"

"Yes, I didn't care for him."

"Now, did he have thin blonde hair?"

"Yes."

"That was Ned. How about the other guy?"

"You mean the handsome guy?"

"Yes."

"He was fine."

Ned agreed with my scenario took a little umbrage about his thinning hair and real laughter about me being handsome.

"You're right, remind me if I start in please, and stop me.

We arrived and drove through the gates attached to a long fieldstone wall on both sides, up a long drive with magnificent grounds to the house. Waiting for us was the maintenance man, a young islander typical of the area, trustworthy diligent, quiet, just the type you would expect and want on your own property. We introduced ourselves as he unlocked the door; we stepped in to a fine not overly ostentatious house with wonderful ocean views of Frenchman's Bay and the Cranberry Islands.

"I would be happy to show you around the house or I can be nearby if you have any questions."

"We're fine on our own," said Ned.

"All right, this is the kitchen, it leads to the dining room, which in turn leads to the sunken living room and the upstairs quarters are accessed by the stairway off to your right."

"Great," says Ned, "We'll start in."

Well, the kitchen tour was extensive. The ceiling was good, the cabinets were good, and the floor was excellent. Overall, it was done in good taste.

"Dick" whispered Ned, "Look at the counter top."

I was across the room and didn't hear his request. Foolishly I said in louder tones, "What?"

He responded in louder tones, "The counter top doesn't work."

I put my finger up to my lips since the young man was in the next room. Ned made his shameful kid's face and covered his mouth with his hands. We continued into the dining room and went through with a fine-tooth comb. He made a few nice loud comments and several whispered denigration's in my ear.

In the living room, which I thought was done in good taste, he began to wax hot over things he didn't like. "Dick," no pretense at secrecy any longer, "this fireplace is a disaster."

I went to shush him up again, but I could see it was a lost cause.

"Freshwater isn't going to do that in my house, Jesus Christ he doesn't have a clue, and the guy who designed the woodwork ought to go to jail."

I couldn't help but to begin to laugh. Ned Johnson isn't used to being shushed up. We went upstairs and the floors had been painted green. Ned stuck his tongue out and pretended to puke. I couldn't stop laughing at this point. He made faces so comedic at everything he could have gone on the English stage.

The rest of the tour continued that way. Thank goodness, it was shortly to end. We started back down the stairs to the first floor. I said I thought the banister was nice. He turned to me and gave me the "cut throat" sign. I broke up; I had to get out.

We thanked the young man and got in the truck. Nothing was said until we had cleared the property.

"Did I do all right in there?" he added.

"Oh yeah," said I, "you were great." I could not look at him. I could not stop laughing. The tears came out of my eyes.

"Was I overly critical?"

"A little." I gagged.

"Well, why the hell didn't you stop me?"

"I couldn't!" I replied.

"Oh well, he is just the maintenance guy. He's not going to cause us any trouble."

Well, a couple of months later we began to plan a pagoda, a real one on his property overlooking the lake. High on a hill called by now Pagoda Hill. It was a remnant or deposit of gravel about thirty feet high left by the last glacier eighteen thousand years ago when it had receded and scooped out Long Pond.

The legal height on the pond for a building that close to the water was forty feet. Naturally, Ned wanted it to be forty-eight feet. That meant I would have to again go to the planning board for approval, which I didn't want to do. They were sick of me.

I decided to stage a platform on the hill, get him up top, and let him see the view at forty feet, maybe averting another blood bath (my blood) at the town hall. I had the men anchor and erect the staging about four stories high. He didn't know until he and Lilly came up one weekend for minor things that we had a staging, a hoisting wheel up top, a boson chair and plenty of one-inch nylon rope. We weren't taking any chances with our valuable cargo. We rigged it all up and tried it with one of the heavy guys. It worked to perfection. On Saturday, we were ready to hoist the chairman to the platform. We had four woodsmen, two carpenters, Lilly and Ned, and me. We were dressed for winter snows and chilling winds as we trudged through a foot of freshly fallen snow.

The staging was a surprise to the Johnson's. They were amazed at this apparition in the woods. Ned could hardly wait to get started. He proceeded to knock the snow off his boots in the clearing and started for the staging ladder.

"Hold on Ned," I said.

"What?"

"You can't climb four stories without some safety devices."

"Aw, cut it out, I'm on my way."

"Ned please, please don't start taking chances. This tower is forty feet high. That's the height of a four story building."

Lilly piped up, "Ned, listen to Dick. He has a plan."

He gave in and we fitted him into the sling chair. We connected him and his chair to the rope that ran to the top and back down the pulley system.

"Are we ready?" says Ned.

"Yes, start climbing." I turned to the two guys on the ropes and said keep just a light tension so he'll get the feeling of climbing freely.

Things went well going up and Wayne Merchant our tree cutter, helped hoist Ned over the top rail. The two of them looked out over the view and had a five-minute discussion.

"Dick?"

"What?"

"It's a great view of the pond and the Twin Mountains. You wouldn't know if you were in Japan or Maine."

"Wow that's great!"

"I think we need that extra eight feet."

Aw shit, I thought, here we go again. "That means fighting with the planning board again." I replied.

"Yep, but as you always say to me 'if its worth doing, it's worth doing well.' Remember that?"

Glumly I replied, "Yep."

He climbed over the top rail with Wayne's help and started down.

"Give me some slack!" he yelled.

I softly said to the men, "keep the tension on that rope," and they did.

"God damn it Dick I heard that. I want some slack so I can climb myself!"

I said, "Give him a little, maybe three feet or so."

He came down about ten feet, doing well on his own, when he hit ice on the step rail and slipped. Not badly, but enough to get hurt if he hadn't been roped. He dangled and the men had reacted quickly. He recovered his composure, reached out and caught the side rail, and finished under the restraint of the rigging. Nobody said a thing, but when he landed and was getting out of the sling, he took a side-glance at Lilly and I to see our reaction. We didn't react.

"Lilly," he said, "It's fun. Would you like to go up?"

"No thanks."

"Dick, why don't you go up?"

"I don't care to." I replied.

"Why not?" he asked.

"It's dangerous and I fear heights."

Everybody starts laughing. Ned says "Geez, and you made me do it."

"Yes, we figured you were expendable."

A few days later, we put a permit in for a forty-eight foot Pagoda - one that you could go into and contemplate your navel or something, at about one million dollars a pop.

The planning board met on Thursdays and I dutifully showed up with my pagoda plan. When it was my turn, I approached the board, laid the plan on the table, and waited for their reaction.

I knew the first guy to react after a few minutes of study would be Farnum Butler. He was about eighty four, could play tennis, produced boats of his own design, had a degree from Harvard, which he had ignored when in his youth, he returned to his beloved island and made a great success of the Butler Boatyards. He was calamitous at town meetings and said exactly what he thought. I knew I was in trouble when he looked up after a few minutes and said, "Listen, what in the hell do you need eight more feet for? Can't you get along with a forty-foot pagoda?"

I responded, "All I can tell you is he knows his pagodas, as well as you know boats. He says in order to make it look right he needs eight more feet."

"Aw crap." he says.

I had devised an argument, but it was a weak one. I had to try it, but I wasn't in a good defensive position, and Farnum and the rest knew it.

"Farnum, you know boat designs, you know when the design is not balanced and is either too long or too short, and it doesn't have the look of a Butler boat, or a Hinckley." He knew I was lathering him with butter, but we were friends and he allowed me to continue and make a fool of myself.

He looked down at the table, as did the others, while I poured on the bullshit. Finally, he held up his hand and said, "For God's sake, if this guy Johnson didn't have more money than brains, we wouldn't even be considering this. I'm voting against it. How about the rest of you fellas?" They nodded.

Now, what goes around comes around as the saying goes, and the board chairman opened his stamp box, wet the stamp good in red ink, and slammed "REJECTED" on the petition with what appeared to me to be almost an insulting enthusiasm. I looked closely at him and who was it but the young maintenance man who had given us the tour of Rockefeller Jr.'s house.

I slunk off into the night.

Shortly after the pagoda disaster, or public relations disaster I guess, we had another incident that followed that winter. Just outside the hot tub, we had a tremendous grove of trees. There were about eight or ten of the huge things. Trees protect each other. When you get high winds they seem to have set-up a protective barrier, so the big trees are guarding the weaker trees in back. One of those trees can suck up 40 gallons of water in one day. You know they don't talk, but if one tree gets a disease out in front the other trees start bleeding a substance to prevent the disease from carrying over to the grove. Anyway, I went down to Florida in late 1996 early 1997 just for a week or two. While I was gone, lo and behold, we had 80 to 90 mile an hour winds and it took down, I call it the "Father Tree – the Protector Tree." When that went down it took about four others in back. The wind continued and it blew down about five more trees. They were just like match sticks. We had an awful mess out there. I came back to begin the clean up.

We had shut down for the weekend to give Lilly and Ned some peace. We had been going seven days a week.

On Friday, Ned and I walked over to the disaster area.

"What the hell happened here?'

"A small local hurricane."

"I know, you told me on the phone, but why after so many years does a whole grove go over?"

I said, "We changed the wind lines. When we removed trees for the expanded foundation we must have taken the big brother down leaving the others exposed."

"What's the plan?"

"On Monday the crew will be in to clean it up, however, if you'll look down here, you'll see our main problem." In a ditch one hundred feet down stream from the house, a torrent of water was pouring out at exactly where we had planned the septic tank and hot tub foundation.

"Oh brother," says Ned, "what the hell are we going to do about that?"

"We've got to find it under the slope, or the hill up back. The problem is it's deep underground and we haven't any idea where it's hiding."

"How come we're not working tomorrow?"

"I figured you'd like it quiet."

"Not me. Let's see. Will Tater come in with a crew?"

"He will."

"Call him up," says Ned, "lets see if we can solve the water problem."

He loved this kind of stuff. I called Tater and he called his crew and several carpenters, about eight guys plus Ned and me. The following morning men and equipment poured into the construction area. Ned was waiting with a big grin. Tater laughed with joy (thinking of the overtime). I said nothing (thinking of the overtime) and the budget (shot to hell anyway).

Earlier that morning a friend of Ned's had called and wanted to visit with Lilly and Ned. Answering the phone as I waited and Ned got dressed (we were all living together in the cottage), Lilly yelled, "Ned, it's George so and so," as Ned approached the phone Lilly put her hand over the speaker and said, "I don't want them over here, Ned. I don't want to entertain them, please."

With Edward leaning over the loft railing saying "Yeah Dad," Ned picked up the phone and said "Hi George, come on over. We're working on a big problem." He hangs up and Lilly says, "Ned!" in exasperation. Edward says "Dad!" in exasperation. Sarah and I turned away and busied ourselves, or buried our amusement in trivia. Sure enough over came George and his beautiful German girlfriend. Lilly was cool. Edward stayed upstairs in a sulk. Ned and I took them away to the problem area. Sarah went shopping.

Dave Blanchard showed up, soon to be appointed caretaker, and joined the group standing around trying to solve the problem. You could spend all day with two back hoes, grubbing and mucking around, and still not find the underground source of the stream.

Dave suggested we call in the local shaman, who also was a dowser, and see if that would work. Ned and I looked at him with sarcastic mutterings of disdain. George and his girlfriend laughed as they sat on the edge of the foundation amused at the dilemma. Dave walked off into the woods and came back shortly with a dowsing rod he had cut and shaped from the proper tree branch. "Anyone want to try this? Anyone feeling like a witch or a magician?" Nobody volunteered, so he started walking up the hill with both hands on the dowsing stick shaped like a "Y" with the single branch level in front of him and a light grip on the horns. Ten minutes went by and nothing happened. In the meantime, we had been laying out a grid for Tater to start probing with the machinery.

David came back and tossed the stick onto the ground. "I haven't got it and never did, but I've seen it done and it's incredible." Well, of course Ned saunters over, picks up the stick, and starts fooling with it. All I can think of is if it ever worked for him we would have a public relations disaster on our hands.

He starts up hill in a trance-like attitude goes about thirty yards and yells, "Dick, Dick!"

"What?"

"This God damn thing is pulling itself right at the ground. Jesus Christ, come here."

Well Jesus wasn't anywhere around, so I went up. "Are you kidding?"

"No, no, look!"

I marked the spot with a stone and my heel. We have to humor him, so I yelled at Tater to bring up a backhoe and start digging. The men stood around grinning. I have mixed emotions. I wanted to find the stream, but I didn't need a mystic for a boss, and neither did Fidelity.

Nine feet down, right under the spot he had found we struck the flowing stream dead center. Everyone except me cheered "Our hero, our dowser, our own magician." All I could think of was headlines in the Boston papers; *"Ned Johnson Turns To Dowsing, Fund Managers Fear For Jobs, Vanguard And Schwab Stocks Lose Liquidity And The Market's Underwater."*

We dug a channel 30 feet long, brought in some pipe and fittings, and diverted the stream past the septic systems and the hot tub area and back downstream into it's channel and on to the lake. Ned stood around with his stick occasionally asking if we needed more dowsing, maybe all the way to the lake if we wanted to. He would be happy to oblige. We, meaning Tater and me, knew we had created a monster. Never again would he take our advice.

In the spur of the moment, between amazed amusement on our part and righteous vindication on his, I made everybody stop working, line up in front of the foundation, including George and his German girlfriend and swear they would never reveal this to any newspaper or magazine, including the "Berlin Zeitgung" on pain of death or loss of all mutual funds, or even bonds. They swore with right hands raised in laughter and we never had a problem until right now. I gave the oath, I didn't take it.

Ned lost his stick. It was sad over the next few months to see him wandering late in the day in the woods with the wrong stick, lost and bewildered until Lilly called him in for cocktails and dinner. Ned was a hollow man without his power of dowsing. He began to drink more wine and much to our dismay, he no longer swam, drank water, or sprinkled the flowers. Nothing worse than a dowser gone dry, lost confidence.

The phone rings late in the evening at the guesthouse in Maine. I pick it up. I know who it is. He's just back from China with Tara. "Hello?"

"Well hello" (emphasis on lo).

"Hi Ned. How are you?"

"Just fine, just fine."

"A good trip?"

"Pretty good. Tara and I found some things we could use in Maine. Some things for the Peabody (a museum)."

"Nice."

"I was gone about three weeks I guess, but I had a problem at the airport and I was afraid I was going to be there a lot longer."

"What happened?"

"Well you know these Chinese want an arm and a leg for everything they don't need, or don't consider valuable and heaven knows I pay damn good money for the stuff we find, then we pay an export tax at the port of embarkation."

"Yes. You've mentioned this before."

"Well, I got a little fed up with all these taxes, so when I bought two little ancient figurines I just slipped them in my jacket pocket. One on each side figuring they'd check my luggage. They always do and not bother with me."

I thought to myself, oh brother; he's a guy who can't get away with anything. He can't help but look guilty.

"Anyway they caught me. Took me into an empty room relieved me of the little statues and conducted a thorough search."

"Jesus Ned."

"Yeah, well they put me in jail for the night. I missed the plane and I didn't get anything to eat." All I could think of was the headline in the Boston Globe *"Ned Johnson Jailed in China"* followed by an article by Steve Bailey, Ned's only friend on the newspaper, stating the reason Steve's mutual funds have dropped is because Ned had headed up a huge smuggling ring in China and wasn't paying attention to business.

"What finally happened?"

"In the morning they said I could make one call. Believe it or not I thought of calling you because you're street smart and probably could handle these Chinese policemen, but I called the American Consul and he explained who I was and they let me go with a fine, but kept the figurines.

"Geez, I'm glad you didn't call me. I hate Chinese food. We'd probably both still be in jail."

CHAPTER 15 – TINKERING WITH DYNAMITE

Ned loved gadgets when he was a young boy. His sister remembers some of his inventions. In addition, if you went into his room you wouldn't know what was going to happen to you.

His actions in Maine while we built the various houses told me he had carried this love of tinkering into his later years. While we were measuring grades with laser beam surveying equipment, accurate to a thirty second of an inch, he was down in the thick of things running red, white and yellow strings from a nail in a tree over to a brick on top of the footings, then onto a stick stuck in the ground, etc. He was a pain in the ass. Guys were stumbling or getting wound up in his strings and he would call me off the blasting and drilling project to hold a string in the air while he found a longer stick to replace me, but we liked him so much and he was the owner – we couldn't say anything to hurt his feelings.

One day I found him standing on a high piece of ledge that had been drilled, powdered, and half-wired to the detonator switch. The dynamite guy was holding the signal horn and the wire until he had moved off the ledge I said to him, "What are you standing here for?"

"I'm waiting to see the blast."

"That's fine," I said, "but they won't do it until the horn goes off."

"When's that going to happen?"

"The minute you get off this ledge."

"Jesus, am I holding things up?"

"Yep."

I signaled the blaster to blow the horn and warn everyone to take cover. Ned jumped three feet and started to seek shelter with me. "How long have we got?" he yelled.

Everyone started laughing, of course we wouldn't blow until we were sure all the workers, including him were safe.

He and I got behind a tree about one hundred feet away, but he was always curious and kept poking his head out to watch.

The blaster yelled over to us to inform me he had run out of blasting powder and was using ordinary commercial fertilizer, which is more powerful and unpredictable.

"What does that mean?" asked Ned.

"It means if you stick your head out again, you won't have time to pull it in."

"Jesus Christ!" he says, "Move over and give me a little more room."

They let it go and the blast was a humdinger. Rocks went everywhere including past our tree and out into the woods. That prompted the blaster and me to not use manure again when we ran out of dynamite. Even the blasting mats were damaged.

Later that weekend, Ned began to take an interest in the big Caterpillar Dozers that were working the site. They could knock a good-sized house or barn down in minutes. I remember the first time I saw him quizzing the operators who, like all the tradesmen, were told to respond to any requests or questions he asked about. Anything that was dangerous to him was to be brought to my attention, since I was in charge of the job site and he was a curious guy and a risk taker. I used the power he gave me to keep him under control as well as the rest of them, and I would bring that to his attention when something began to get out of hand.

Ned had world class, number one financial power, but you can't physically see that quality. You can experience the perks like; jet planes, world-class hotels, the best wines and food, international courtesans and so on, but physically these are draining. Hop on a D-10 Dozer, start the diesel engine, throw it into gear, start clanking along on huge treads, pull-up to a pile of dirt that would take ten men a day to move, drop the blade down, move into the pile and hear the diesel pull itself up to snuff, and move the earth. Wow, that's Ned Johnson stuff and here's a chance to use it, feel it, and know what power really feels like as it runs up your arm through your shoulders and into your brain. It could make a maniac out of a madman. It's a mindless form of destruction that serves a purpose, in particular it doesn't talk back or require polite responses.

Tater Grey is fearless with a machine and yet he can drive through the Maine countryside, see a wonderful farm with cows and barns and green grass around a neat white house and start to cry – sit in his truck and cry.

Ned wanted that, but he couldn't have a machine because he would cause millions of dollars worth of damage. We did all we could, hiding keys, draining fuel tanks, disconnecting wires so while we were not there he wouldn't start one up and go off on a toot. He'd be a danger to his neighbors knocking things down. He is clever with gadgets. He is a business savant with childish, yet clever ideas. He is always working on something in his mind. You can't get his attention if he is focused. I have seen it in the family world. It's frightening to see; it's amazing. He goes into a trance no matter who or how many people are in the room, you cannot draw him out, short of physically grabbing him, and I've never seen that done or even tried.

During the telephone wiring and cabling of his house, he sent his expert on those matters to Maine. I did not interfere with the fellow because I didn't know much about the issues. It didn't turn out well. One day while riding in the truck with Ned, with his son Edward in the back seat, he started a tirade on the systems and how lousy they were, and then turned to me and said, "Who the hell did that?"

"I don't remember," I said.

"Are you kidding me? You don't know?"

"Well Ned, I know, but I am not a guy to stool on someone and cost him his job."

His anger at that answer was the worst I had seen since I had become friendly with him.

"I'll find out, God damn it, and heads will roll."

"Hold on," I said, "think about the situation you've put me in."

"I don't give a shit," he said.

Edward sat mute in back in awe of his father's anger.

"Ned, Ned, listen to me please. This guy works for you, was sent up by you and you are responsible for his work, okay?"

He sat and looked out the window, "Oh shit, I know who it is. I didn't think he knew his ass from his elbow, and he's been with us for about fourteen years. Oh shit."

"Now," I said, "you've made a stool pigeon out of me."

"I apologize. I'm sorry. I didn't think it through."

Edward sat back. I sat back and we drove home in silence. The guy four years later still works at Fidelity in a lighter capacity.

CHAPTER 16 – THE HOUSE AND PICNIC BOAT

The main house was going up, we had poured the foundations, etc., and we had Bond builders going good. He got that first deck on. Once he got that on, I called Tater Gray and had him come over to back fill around the entire foundation, because it is a lot easier for the workmen to work and for Ned to picture the grounds. We had already waterproofed the foundation in my own self-interest, since I didn't want him to see I had raised the house about two and a half feet after he had agreed to give me only a foot.

In the process of working around with Tater and back filling nicely and raking it out, we got down to the waterfront side and looked at the berm that was there. It was about six feet high with 50-60 year old trees growing out of it. I said to Tater "what the hell is that?"

He said "I think that's the castings that were dug out from the old house in 1927, or there about and I don't see it as permanent landscape." We saw on the other side of the berm that we picked up original landscape and a stream, lovely nice things and a path that goes down to the boathouse.

So I said, "Well, let's get Wayne Merchant the tree cutter." Wayne came over with his men, went up, and topped off three of the big ones. Then he came part way down and topped the rest of them. He got the trees down so all that was left were the stumps. He pulled them out and Tater used a huge bulldozer and took that whole berm down and all the stumps with it. By God, there we were about one foot above the level of the landscape outside and the first step out of the lower level of the building. We were back where we were in 1927, which was a much nicer, prettier and easier landscape to work with. It gave us an opportunity to not only do upper decks for the top floor, but to do lower decks for the lower floor, just one foot above grade.

We raked it all out (there's an old saying up in Maine, it isn't finished until it's raked). We had 14 carpenters, plumbers starting on the undergrounds, and the electricians wiring. At one point, we had 48 pickup trucks in the yard and all types of equipment working. It was a joy to see. I thought to myself – we have a straight run up unless we get too many change orders from Ned. I think I should tackle the landscape.

Ned had used Patrick Chasse who was very intelligent and a good landscaper on the island. He had done some work for Ned on the little cottage two or three years before. He had done some work around the island for the wealthy. People thought very highly of him and he taught one or two days a week at Harvard. I called Patrick and he came over. I explained to him we had a major project and I wanted him to consider getting involved. He brought with him a young fellow, George Workman, who was working for him and was a landscape architect. Patrick said, "Look, I don't like to work for Mr. Johnson and I don't think I'm going to. I'll tell you why, he doesn't take care of his grounds. He doesn't use the right people. He's too cheap to hire people who know what they are doing. He has a guy who plows his driveway in the winter fooling around with his shrubs. Now, if you look at the landscaping around the guest cottage you will see it's not up to snuff. It's not what it should be and there are a lot of weeds. I'm taking a bit of a hit for it, because he's mad at me since some of the stuff died, it wasn't pruned, treated and fertilized. So he has done a bit of a job on my reputation here on the island and I'm not going to work for him."

Well, I felt bad and in fact, I talked with Ned that night. I said, "You had mentioned Patrick Chasse."

He said, "Yes, Patrick's good, but he's had an awful mortality rate on his plants. He's lost about 40% of them around that cottage."

I said, "You and I always talk pretty plain to each other and that's a good way to be. He's blaming you for not taking care of them."

He said, "Aw, he's full of crap! I don't want him on the property. To hell with him. We shouldn't of had to take care of them. They should of come along by themselves."

I said, "Okay, I'll look for somebody else." We hung up.

The next morning George Workman came over. He asked if we could speak confidentially. He said, "Patrick is thinking of closing up and teaching full time down in Cambridge. I'm working in the office and I don't particularly like the atmosphere. There are two girls there, nothing wrong with that. They don't have a lot of knowledge and I have a hard time getting my work done. I'm thinking of quitting. If I quit, would you hire me and let me work on the landscaping?"

I said, "I'll tell you what I'll do, as long as you make a clean break with Patrick and he's satisfied, I will hire you, but I won't hire you as a full-charge landscaper. I'll hire you to work with Ned Johnson and me. We have our percentage of say in what is going to happen, but you certainly would be helpful in identifying species and plants, things like that survive up here in the north." So he did. He went back and spoke to Patrick who approved of his move.

George came aboard and I put him on an hourly design basis to start, in which he would bill us by the hour for his board work. The next couple of weeks we went over a lot of stuff. In fact, Ned came up and joined in. He liked George. He said "Fine. You keep an eye on him and so will I."

I said, "Fine, I think he's a bright young man and he's got some good ideas."

That's what we did in the course of landscaping around the house. Ned wanted to have a private road built way out on the boundary line. We now call it the road to nowhere, but it really comes down off the main road and runs fairly close to the boathouse. It's a wonderful road. George designed it. We had the environmental people come in because we had some swamplands to cross. Instead of building bridges, they let us build stone bridges, which we did and saved some money. George landscaped the road in a primitive way so it blended in with the woods. He got almost 100% growth out of it the first couple of years, because we kept after it. We had a guy who came in and fertilized and trimmed on a regular schedule.

Bond is moving the house up. Bill McHenry and Brian Reading are designing special things for Ned. For example, in the kitchen – all Corian tops, Corian center station. All of the cabinets to be made out of Douglas Fir. The finest Douglas fir in the world is out in the state of Washington and they had a tree out there they were going to cut. They were going to mill about half of it for the US Constitution decking in Boston and the other half was for sale. We bid on it and got the other half, or enough of it to do what we wanted to do. It was shipped cross-country. Beautiful stuff. We stored it in an old boathouse. Bond's men went there with trucks, took pieces of it, and began to fabricate the Fir cabinets out of this wonderful tree, which was 1100 years old by the rings. We made dividing doors out of it that divided the dining room with the kitchen. Wonderful contraption. You folded up the doors or you could close the doors completely, and have one on the right and one on the left that would swing open one way or the other. Alternatively, you could go with half doors, or you could fold them all up and slide them into the wall – one to the left and one to the right. No doors there at all, which is the way it was used in general.

When we had chefs and cooks there we could set it up so the whole wall was closed except one door, which would open either way and they would come through there to serve dinner. In the dining room, we had ordered Alaskan Yellow Cedar. Ned wanted to get some of it before the Japanese got it all. So, we got an agent out in British Columbia who went out and selected all knotless, Alaskan Yellow Cedar, absolutely beautiful wood. Joe Tracy flew out and the Bear Creek Lumber Company in Washington milled it. Joe approved most, rejected some. They shipped that on a trailer cross-country. We stored it in another warehouse on the island.

What we were going to do, we finally found out, was a wood ceiling in the living room and dining area with a Japanese/Chinese motif. Ned had selected, unknown to us, U-Sing Jung from Jung Brannen to come up and do the design. At that point, we had three architects, one interior designer, one interior decorator, two curators, and George working with landscape. We were pretty well staffed.

U-Sing came up and did a lot of measuring on the dining room and living room ceiling, which was about 28 by 45. He then went back to his shop in Boston and designed the ceilings for the house. The question came up, "Is there any woodworker in Maine who can do this work as well as a guy in New York who Ned knew, or another firm in Boston that makes elegant dining room tables?" I called Joe Tracy who had a little shop up here. He had done quite a bit of work for the Rockefellers, the Hudson's and out on the island of Frenchboro for a guy by the name of Butler. Joe wanted to take me out to the island, which we eventually did. I thought Joe was pretty good. I showed him the plans when we finally got them up from Boston. I asked, "Can you build this?"

He said "Yep."

I asked, "How long will it take you Joe?"

He said, "Leave the plans here."

He's walking around in sawdust. He's got about four guys working in sawdust. He's a casual guy. He makes cider every year. He's a great sailor. He can take a sailboat and go about anywhere. He makes his own boats slim and shiny circa 1928. Beautiful work.

A couple of days later Joe called and said, "I don't see any problem with this, but I think it's going to take a year to do it."

I said, "Well, you better get started on it and I'll talk with Ned." So that night I called Ned and said, "We've got a guy who can do this work."

He said, "I don't think so."

"I'm telling you I am going out with him this week and see Gil Butler's house out on this island. I'll look at it and I'll let you know."

" Okay."

A couple of days later Joe hired a lobsterman to take us out to the island and see Gil Butler's house, which he built from scratch. We landed in this wonderful little cove and got off the boat. The guy says, "I will pick you up in about three hours, that's when I have to make a run back." Joe and I went up the hill around a little church across the bay. There were a couple of little boathouses on the side we were on and a little dock. This was one of the most charming islands, little houses on it. There was a family, the Lunts, who had been there for a couple of hundred years. We walked through this gate onto Gil Butler's property and immediately flushed about six deer, which ran down toward the ocean. Joe and I walked down this curving dirt road and the first thing I saw was a Japanese Bridge. We crossed over that, and then came to a magnificent teahouse that had all types of special woods in it. Joe had taken Birch trees and sliced the bark off them and made wallpaper out of it. It looked so real. He had done all the cabinetry, the bedrooms, and the floors. I think he had moved his shop out there and worked about six years. I was very impressed. His artistry was as good as his craftsmanship.

We went back with the lobsterman and I called Ned that night. I said, "Ned, this is our guy."

He said, "I am telling you those guys up there are good. I know they are good. They work for Hinckley and they do all this and that, but I can't take a chance."

"Ned, this guy trained for years in a woodworking shop. He is a master carver and woodworker. He's worked for all of the big families."

"All right, I'm coming up. I want to see him. I want to go out to Butlers."

We arranged for Ned to come up. He and Lilly flew up at night into the airport at Bar Harbor. I picked them up as I did many a night in the hot weather, cold, snow, or whatever. They would fly in anything. Some people would get off the plane and they were all absolutely green or throwing up, and they're sitting there and didn't know they had landed. He would be working with his computer and she was reading.

They got in and we got them straightened around in the guest cottage. Of course, we were living there at the time. The next morning I got a call from Joe," Hinckley has offered a picnic boat." Now picnic boats are $500,000.00 new.

"Joe there is no way in the world Ned Johnson is going to buy a picnic boat. I know what Hinckley is trying to do. I appreciate it, but I just want to keep it simple. Get the lobsterman for $50.00 and away we go."

He said, "No, they want to do it. They said they would meet us at Bass Harbor and wait for us and take us out. There would be a skipper there, and he'll wait and bring us back."

"Okay, but tell them no dice on a sale."

The next morning we arrived at Bass Harbor and there was a beautiful 38-foot twin Diesel Jet Picnic boat. It had a draft of about 10 inches. It slept two, but the technology and workmanship were outstanding. We boarded and Joe said, "I think he's interested."

I said, "Joe, he's not interested."

"Okay."

We go out and Joe is up front with the skipper. Ned and I are sitting back near the burgee pole. He said, "What a day. I am so glad we are doing this. Isn't this wonderful? This is quite a little boat."

I said, "Yes it is. It's a nice boat. It's a new design called a Hinckley Picnic Boat. I think its hull #53." A few minutes later Joe came back. Now Joe had no interest in this. Joe is just a guy who liked to have rich people buy nice boats, then maybe he would get a chance to ride in them. He came back, had all the literature, and laid it down on the seats in the back. Ned looked at them, but not too interested.

Finally, we arrived in Frenchboro. We circled around the little inner harbor, very quiet. Pulling up to this rickety old dock, we tied her up and jumped off. The skipper was a nice young fellow. He said, "I'll wait here. It's a beautiful day, no hurry." We left and went up a circular type hill. You had to walk backwards practically before you could take a hairpin turn to start up the hill, get over, and look down the other side.

When we took the hairpin turn, we were now looking down on the boat. Ned stopped and said to me, "Now isn't that a sight. Now isn't that pretty. Look at that boat sitting in that beautiful dark blue green water."

I looked at Joe who grinned and said to myself "Uh oh."

We went to Butlers. Ned loved it. He loved Joe. He just couldn't get over him. I think Joe is superb and he is comfortable with anybody. We walked back. We were at the top of the hill again. Ned framed the boat like a photographer or an artist and says isn't that beautiful. Down we go and board the boat. We untie her and pull in the lines and the bumpers, and start back about 10 to 12 miles towards Bass Harbor. Now, Ned is up front with the skipper, and Joe and I are back near the Burgee pole.

We're sitting there and Joe turns to me with a big shit-eating grin and says "Well, I think you and I are going to have a lot of fun with this boat. He won't have the time, so we'll use it."

We got back to Bass Rocks and climbed the ladder up onto the dock and Ned watched the Hinckley pull out and get on line back to the Hinckley dockyards, which were in Southwest Harbor on the other side of the island. I was driving the truck and dropped Joe off at his shop. He went in and went back to work. Ned and I went back to the cottage. Lilly and Sarah were waiting. We walked in the door and sat down and Sarah made us lunch, and Lilly helped.

He says, "Now you know what I'm thinking? I'm thinking this isn't really fair to Lilly. Here I've got this beautiful home being built." Of course, it was being built for Lilly too. In addition, we had by this time acquired a house for Edward that hadn't been fixed up yet. He says, "Edward has just bought a beautiful home on the water, and I think, Lilly, you ought to have something."

She says, "Well, what do you think I ought to have?"

"I think you ought to have a picnic boat."

"Oh wouldn't that be fun" says Lilly.

So, he picks up the phone and calls the young fellow at Hinckley's and says, "You know, I liked that boat so well, I think I'll have one."

"All right," says the fellow. "Do you want to come down and go over it?"

"Yep," he says. "I'll be down with my son, Edward, next week, but I will put the order in now. You can start putting me in line for the hull." Of course, this wasn't a sailboat. It was a powerboat, but Edward was a good boatman. "We'll come down and we'll go all over the specs and put in the stuff we want. We want everything in it."

Edward's property had been purchased just before the boat. As we walked along on Ned's property, Ned had said to me "I want you to do me a favor. I want you to look for something for Edward. He likes to charter big 65 and 70 foot sailboats and it would be awful nice if he had his own place up here."

I said, "Well, it would be, but I would think you would want to be on the ocean, and you're not on the ocean, you're on a lake."

He says, "Yeah, I think you better look for something on the ocean."

I said, "Fine. I'll call a real estate dealer and have her give me a hand." I had somebody in mind; it was Janet Moore. She was working for Train Company at the time, but later went into business for herself, and I mentored her a little to help her.

I called her up and met with her in the office on site. She came over – a very pleasant person with a nice personality, a go-getter. I said, "I want to buy a piece of property on the water. I would like to buy it in the pretty marsh area. Mr. Johnson and his son don't want to be down on Seal Harbor, or anywhere near the socialites. He prefers the quiet side of the island," which was Pretty Marsh, "and Bartlett Landing." If you circle around Bartlett Island you go on out to Blue Hill Bay. It's only about an hour's ride down to Blue Hill Bay. The town itself is pretty and there are more artists, antiques and things to see than there is in Ellsworth, which is the nearest town to Bar Harbor. Bar Harbor is a tourist Mecca. It's not as tacky as some, in fact, I think it's a great town, and they have had as many as 60 cruise ship visits a season.

We began a search for a home for Edward as we continued to build the house for Ned. The interior designs were being done while we were roughing out the house and Ned of course, had come up and was delighted with the lower level. Nothing was ever mentioned about the extra foot and a half, because it worked out so well. Except later in years he would point at me and say, "I know you raised that house a foot and a half more than I gave you."

I got George Workman going on the landscape and we had the interior being designed, but there were many changes. He wanted a column here; he didn't want a column there. We had to put in a lot of steel. We had to prepare for the two ceilings that were going to go in the dining room and living room. Change orders began to come-in in a steady flow. His phone calls increased. In the two and half years it took me to build this house and do Edward's, and Pray's Meadows where I lived, I know I received over 500 phone calls. He was so interested. Sometimes people try to reach him for days, businessmen from all the companies and they can't get to him. I could get to him with one phone call. That's how much he loved building. If I didn't call him, he usually called me.

After a couple of hundred phone calls I wasn't surprised at anything. You might get a phone call on Tuesday at 6:30 from a limousine, then again on Wednesday at 9:00 and he's in the bathtub. Calls are one thing, but you also are going to get ten questions. I don't know where he ever came up with them all, and you've got to have ten answers. I began to feel like Scheherazade telling the Arabian Sheik the stories of 1,001 nights. If the time came that she didn't have a story to tell, she'd have to be put away. I had such a deep interest and a love for the work I was doing, I was able to handle the phone calls and give him his answers to the ten questions, and I know there was ten – a total of about 5,000 questions in two and half years. He knew as much about the job as I did. His functioning style was audio and mine was visual, but he knew a lot about his building, and he changed it and changed it.

Sometimes we did the work over twice and when we occasionally did it three times the carpenters would complain. I said, "I know he is making a lot of changes. We are dealing with a very talented eccentric man. He does pay you."

And they said "Oh yeah, no, no, we know we are getting paid. That isn't the point. We don't mind doing the work twice Dick, but when we start to do it three and four times it gets a little tiring. It gets a little boring."

I said, "All right. Stay with me. I'll try to minimize it. I'll try to spread the work around. You do something and he wants to change it, I'll put another carpenter on it and let him change it. I'll get you away from that syndrome." I didn't blame them.

Well, the owner mandated change orders, which poured in. All of the trim and all doors were hand made. Ned designed the trim. He designed the ceilings. We finished and he decided to coif every ceiling, which means he didn't want them to run square into the wall, he wanted them to curve. We had to go through every single room, both levels and coif the ceilings. We had to lay all the wood floors down in a certain direction when we were finishing, Feng Shui. We read books on the subject. Imagine a bunch of carpenters and a project manager standing there reading and laying the floors in the direction we thought would be appropriate. It turned out we were right. It turned out the carpenters spent the rest of the year telling all of their friends and neighbors they were working Feng Shui with an air of superiority.

The upper level had a kitchen, dining room, living room, library, and master bedroom with a bath and two guest bedrooms with baths. Off the living room is a library with a high ceiling and a lot of down lights. All of the rooms on the upper level have their own decks. In fact, all the rooms in the lower level have sliding doors out onto cracked ice decks and walkways. The master bedroom has a unique ceiling with different sloping angles and some pin lights put in, which would later be used to highlight three Chippendales (the furniture, not the dancers) worth more than the house. The master bedroom has a sliding glass door out onto a private deck overlooking the grounds. The library has its own deck that connects onto the living room deck that connects onto the dining room. This deck connected onto the kitchen deck and around to the side door.

The decks were made of Ipey. Ipey is a Brazilian wood that has fallen into the Amazon River and lain there maybe a hundred years, or better. It's become a source of revenue for the Brazilian lumber companies because it is impervious now to just about anything. You don't even paint it. You might lightly sand it, but you don't paint it. We laid the deck and we couldn't nail it. We had to screw it. Before we could screw it, we had to drill it. When we drilled it, of course, we had to recess above the screw so we could put a bung in it. Bungs were used in Medieval times to close wine casks. These were small bungs and we had 13,000 of them. They all had to be made, treated, punched into the deck and lightly sanded.

I thought we were never going to finish the deck. We had two carpenters on it and they must have been there months. Is the deck magnificent? Yes. Is it impervious to everything? Yes. Will it last forever? Yes. The whole house might collapse, but the deck will be standing.

The master bedroom was designed around a very valuable antique rug, which had a lot of yellow in it. The drapes and so forth were yellow Damask, which picked up the colors in the rug. A long bathroom serves the master bedroom. It was very simply done with some elegant German faucets that weighed ten pounds apiece. Turn to the right and there is a dressing room with special cabinetry that is hand made. Ned laid out the dressing room so he could go in, open his bureau drawers, and if he bent over, he wouldn't bump into Lilly because hers were at the other end on the opposite side. She could open hers without bumping into him. In addition, Ned had Quaker pegs all over the place. The guy is absolutely nuts about Quaker pegs.

Leaving the master bedroom area and going out into a wonderful hallway, that leads down to two guest bedrooms to the right, are four sliding glass doors all done with sixteen light glass windows leading out to part of the cracked ice path that would lead out to the front door. On your left was a beautiful banister that Ned designed with the woodworker, one of Bond's men. Hanging there, when we did finish it, is a light fixture by Tiffany, more on this item later.

You go down the corridor and come to two guest bedrooms. One on the left with a full bath and a door that you can close and then you have your bath, bedroom, and your own private deck looking out on the side. I call it Fox Run, because we always had red foxes out there. In fact, sometimes they would even come up and sit on the deck. They called this the Bermuda room because of the Bermuda furniture and some great artwork. Every time I went into the house, I had to go look at one picture. It had a pin light over it showing two men who looked like they had just arrived at the Mississippi River with a horse and cows, circa 1750 and the horse had just quenched his thirst, drops of water falling from its mouth into the river. I can't describe it. I used to stand there in awe of it.

Then you come out of that set of quarters and go into another set, which also had a door and a hallway with a bathroom that separated that bedroom from the rest of the house. They had a canopy bed in there. They had a chest in there by Hepplewhite and that is what the room is called. The bedroom also has it's own private deck looking out onto a lawn featuring a Japanese Katsura tree that turns silver in the late fall.

Coming back out you go down a circular stairway to the right past two bathrooms and into the hot tub area, a hexagonal room, all glass. When it was all done, Ned came up one weekend and said to me "You know what – I would like that to be raised up about three feet."

I said, "Why?"

He said, "That way when you sit in the hot tub you can look outside." It was an octagonal room with eight doors. I didn't want to change that thing. It was all up and running.

I said "Ned, you can sit in that thing right now and look over the edge and see the grass and everything."

He said "No, no. Let's get our bathing suits." So, we got our bathing suits and put them on and went in and sat down. He was right. You could see the grass, but you didn't get a really good view of the grounds.

I said, "Okay" and we raised it.

Joe Tracy did a cover. It was a miracle of engineering. Ned wanted a cover that he could fold up and put away, but he also wanted to be able to walk on it. I asked "How the hell are we going to be able to do that across an eight foot hot tub." Joe engineered it and got special materials – space age materials – and by God he engineered it so it could be folded into three pieces; two half-round and one square with rounded ends. We had a closet built so you could slide it in and hide it.

I said, "I still don't know why you want that or why you want to be able to walk on it."

"Well, what if we had a party down here and two people got drunk and wanted to fool around."

I said, "Cut it out Ned. Let them go into one of the bedrooms." Anyway, he wanted it raised, so we did it.

Coming back into the house from the hot tub area there is a bedroom with four big sliding glass doors, which I thought was the prettiest room in the house. The room has four stationary and four sliding glass doors. This room looks out on Fox Run and out at the lake on the other side. Around all of this of course, is a cracked ice walk made out of Deer Isle Granite. Ned took his mother and father's bedroom set and put it in there. I swear he put the same quilts and so forth they'd had on it sixty years ago a little bit like the movie where Orson Wells keeps his sled, Rosebud. I began to think that was what I was dealing with. In fact, I knew I was. He kept a lot of old, old keepsakes in a warehouse in Boston, including his father's car. "Citizen Kane" was the movie; Ned Johnson was the real thing.

If you opened the closet door, the lights went on and if you closed them they went off. The hardware was superb. The lighting was indirect. The upstairs ceilings were coifed. Each room had it's own thermostat. Each room had under the floor heat that keeps your toes warm. Then, if you left that bedroom and continued towards the inner part of that lower level you came to the billiard room. The billiard room was a concession to me because I love to play billiards and I thought this would be a heck of a nice thing to play when the son-in-laws come up, and Ned's up and Edward's up – we could have quite a tournament, which we did.

Ned tried playing pool, but I think the dyslexia threw off his coordination. He was discouraged and quit. Edward and I played Chris and Rob, I think we out played them the first time and they out thought us the second time for a draw.

The family room next to the billiard room was off a long beautifully decorated hall; double doors are recessed and generally left open. The right side as you enter has a stunning fireplace that Lilly had decorated with ceramic tiles of frogs, fish, birds, and natural scenes.

The mantle is a block of cherry, very simple. The room and cabinetry are all cherry done by one carpenter, Dave Poland the best.

On the left side is a ping-pong table that can be reconfigured several different ways for storage, practice, or displaying art works. The table itself is a Joe Tracy special. Twelve thousand dollars and when Jim Curvey played on it, he ordered one for his house. The room is filled with lovely contemporary furniture, game tables, and at the far end all glass with two sliding doors out to a deck on a grade of Deer isle granite. The remainder of the lower level consists of a children's refreshment area, a caterer's kitchen, the boiler room, and the electrical room. Both of which could run a small naval cruiser with all sorts of equipment.

From that area there is a set of stairs leading up to a pantry with freezer, then back into the kitchen. The house flows well thanks to all the architects.   The workmanship is temple quality inside and out with only two major mistakes that nobody in the family knows about.

On the outside over the main entrance door there is a three-sided roof with Chinese chain downspouts. The rainwater flows through two copper lined valleys. The carpenters when flashing these valleys made a mistake they are twice as wide as they should be. When we caught it the shingling and roof had been completed. I didn't have the heart to rip it all out, so I let it go in the hope Ned wouldn't notice it and he hasn't to this date.

The other mistake is major and was picked up by U Sing Jung on final ceiling inspections. I knew about it when we started in the dining room with U Sing and Ned. I had mentioned it to Architect Bill McHenry. He didn't comment and appeared to shrug it off at the time.

The dining room and living room ceilings were made of Alaskan Cedar and in their simplicity, they are works of art. They were built to compliment each other.

The problem is the dining room ceiling is offset and not centered to coordinate the design of the living room to flow into each other. In other words, they don't line up and are not continuous.

U Sing spotted this and turned to me to protest. I showed horror in my eyes, which silenced him. He turned back and continued the tour.

Later when we were alone, he said "Dick that's a bad mistake. Can we do something to bring it into the line of Feng Shui?" I replied it would be best to wait, perhaps he would see it and ask for a change, and we could simply call it a change order, rather than start pointing fingers. U-Sing said "You know they'll never be comfortable in that room and it may bring them bad luck." He may have been right. Things haven't gone so well lately. They probably should eat in the kitchen.

CHAPTER 17 – ACQUISITION
ON THE ISLAND

Jan Moore called one night just as Sarah and I were sitting down to supper. This was in November of 1996, early in the game.

"Hi Dick!"

"Hello."

"I think I just hit pay dirt in our search for Edward the 4th's waterfront house."

"Where are you?" I asked.

"I'm standing outside, freezing on the shore at Bartlett Narrows with Gary Fountain, who is a real estate salesman for Hinckley," she answered.

"What have you got?"

"I have eight acres of woods, a two season house with two floors and three hundred gorgeous feet of waterfront on the Narrows looking directly across to Bartlett's Island."

"Wow! I know the area."

"You better come right over," she said.

"Why?"

"There are other parties interested."

"We'll be there in fifteen minutes."

Sarah and I jumped in the car with her checkbook and raced to Narrows Road and onto the property. It was cold, dark, and windy. Jan and Gary stood huddled in the lee of the building. We stopped and got out, even in the dark I could see what a fine piece of property this was, and that it could be made better.

After introductions I walked around the land particularly down to the waterfront, it was perfect. I walked back up to the group. Gary unlocked the door; we went in and walked through the first and second floors. It had a certain charm, but it didn't matter because knowing Edward he would change it all. It was the waterfront, which would give the family access to some of the best sailing waters in the world.

"What's the price?" I asked.

"Six hundred and ninety five thousand."

A bit stiff, I thought, but to me the land was worth more than that.

"I'll take it." I said.

Gary said, "I have a problem with selling it today. I promised two couples, one from Long Island, and one from New Jersey that I would show it to them separately on Saturday. They are flying up."

Sarah was concerned I was trying to buy without showing Edward or Ned. I wasn't.

Jan said nothing; Gary looked at me and said, "if that's all right with you that would be the only conditions."

All I could see from that was we would be participating in an auction.

"That's not all right with me."

"Well, I made a promise." he said.

"Gary."

"Yes."

"Is this property for sale at $695,000.00 at this moment?" I asked.

"Yes."

"Well, under the rules of real estate you are obliged to sell it to me since I have agreed to pay your price."

He gulped a little and said, "Okay."

I said to Sarah, "Give him a one percent check for down payment of earnest money."

Sarah wrote a check for $6,950.00, gave it to Gary, we signed the papers and went home to re-heat our supper.

On Friday night Edward and Ned flew in, I picked them up at the airport on the island and drove right to the property. They got out in the fading light of November in Maine, walked ten steps towards the ocean, turned to me and said, "Fantastic!"

The next day was a bright, but a cold late November morning the three of us met and toured the land, the waterfront, the house and located the lot lines.

They were as thrilled as was I. We could all see the potential. I had gone over the place the day before to confirm the lot lines. I had a surprise for Edward; a gift from the previous owner. The lot lines along the water had been published on the prospective of 300' (+/-). I had taken a tape and measured them on Thursday. We had over 400'(+/-). A gift of 100' of waterfront priced by my standards at two thousand a front foot. That was a two hundred thousand dollar, 'thank you very much' flat out gift from someone who hadn't done their, 'due diligence' very well.

After the official closing weeks later, Edward called and wanted to start on the interior of the house. We brought in Bill McHenry, the architect. He hustled out a set of plans and off we went with Bond Builders again. Eventually we re-did the interior, built a million dollar barn, or close to that, re-did all landscaping, built a dock and a float, against our neighbors wishes (fight still going on), installed all new utilities and wells, and on and on and on.

During the process, Ned tried to dominate Edward's wishes and thoughts. This became a problem for Edward and I who were trying to work together. It got so bad we had to stop Ned and rather than hurt his feelings, we came up with the saying "if you say, you pay."

That slowed him up, but on several occasions, he couldn't control himself. "Oh, Ed don't you think you should bring the electrical services in from narrows Road to the house and barn in an underground trench?"

I said, "We already have service on poles in the woods." Ned ignored me completely.

"Ed, put it underground."

I said, "We'll have to blast near the road. It's all ledge out there." He ignored me completely.

I said, "It will cost $100,000.00."

He ignored me completely and said, "Let's do it," to Ed.

I said, "Remember our agreement, 'if you say you pay.'"

"I don't give a shit," says Ned, "I'll pay for it," and he did.

Numerous other suggestions followed. I can't tell you how much he paid, but it was plenty, and Edward had his own money and legacy, he didn't need these gifts.

When we did the cost controls, we had trouble allocating some large expenditure to the proper person. Be it Ed or Ned who gave and who got. Later, when we were doing legal work against each other, Ned's lawyers decided to investigate a tax problem I had in 1988. It was handled by my CPA to the complete satisfaction of the IRS and concluded in 1997. They dug into it in the hopes of finding something wrong in order to be able to label me as a tax cheat and a liar.

I wonder if Edward paid gift taxes on all the things his father paid for in 1996 and 1997. For some reason, I doubt he did. His tax returns and his father's would be interesting –maybe the pot calling the kettle black.

Jan Moore called again. This time for property being sold that had three hundred feet along Ned's road to nowhere. Also, several hundred feet along Pretty Marsh Road, which was paved and considered one of the main roads on the island. This happened late in the process in the year 2000, the year of my demise. The house belonged to Peg Baily, who also owned property on an island and summered there.

The problem Jan explained was time. Peg was going to get an offer the next morning that was acceptable to her. We needed to move fast if we wanted it. I met with Jan that afternoon, walked the grounds and through the house. It also had a two-car garage and loft. It was a nice home.

"How much?" I asked.

"Two hundred forty five thousand."

It was not worth it to the average buyer and I had doubts she would get a higher offer the next day, but I couldn't take a chance, so I bought it.

I called Patty Hurley. It was about two in the afternoon and explained we had to move fast, to get a check up here and either pay for it, or tie it up. Patty doesn't like doing things like that. The guy who was going to do the check was hesitant. It didn't seem to me I was going to get it done. I started pushing harder. Stepped on some toes I'm afraid and got people going in the right direction, scrambling was something small businesses did to survive. Bureaucracies don't have to, like the wheels of justice, they usually grind slowly along.

All due credit to Patty Hurley and her group. We beat the next offer the next morning by one hour. However, some egos bruise easily and those that do were bruised. I think they felt at Crosby that it was time to circle the wagons, include Ned in the process, and get me out of the loop using retirement or worse. It turned out to be worse.

When Ned was on the stand in Bangor Federal Court one of the questions asked was, "Did Dick Larson participate in purchasing property at all?" Ned's answer, "Yes, he would point things out to me. Things for me and my son, and we would consider them."

I say, "Baloney." I bought without their approval, but within their wishes and it turned out well.

CHAPTER 18 – SOCIAL AND REAL GUY PROBLEMS

Ned Johnson is the world's worst public speaker. He never writes anything down. He never prepares or practices what he is going to say. If he does have a short list of reminder notes, he veers off and never finds his way back. His syntax is worse than Eisenhower's. He talks about the future and mystic things, or subjects the audience doesn't know about. You could be there all night and not know what Ned was talking about!

When William Weld was running for Governor of Massachusetts, he was scheduled to speak to a large audience at the World Trade Center in Boston. The crowd was in and settled on time. Sarah and I were over on the left side of the audience almost out of sight. Weld was late. The crowd got restless. Ned came down our aisle on crutches, the result of a snapped Achilles' heel from tennis. He stopped beside Sarah and me, we were on the end seats, and tapped my foot with his crutch.

"Dick, if he doesn't show up soon, I want you to get up and speak for a while."

"Are you kidding me?"

"No, you are always full of bullshit. You'd do well, so start preparing."

"Oh, I'm all set. I know just what I'm going to say."

"I thought so. What are you going to say?"

"I'm going to tell the audience of your plans to run if Weld doesn't show up."

"Jesus, I'll hit you over the head with my crutch if you do."

"Then you'll fall down and everyone will laugh at you."

"You son a bitch," he said as he limped to the podium. Weld showed a couple of minutes later, thank God.

Ned tries hard to be a regular guy and runs into trouble constantly. He's awkward in a crowd be it social, business or even trying to communicate with guys who worked for us in Maine.

In the early winter of 1998, I got a call from Ned's office. He was on a Colgan air flight from Boston and would land at Bar Harbor at 5:00 p.m. Ned asked for me to please pick him up at that time. I was there at 5:00 p.m., a cold, rainy, windy, early winter night, lousy flying weather, lousy weather to do anything and bad weather predicted all weekend. I was puzzled by the surprise trip, not like him at all. He landed on time came off the plane with a big grin. I was pleased to see him; pleased to see my friend.

"This is a surprise," I said.

"Yeah, I had to get the hell away from the whole thing. Lilly's away, nobody's home."

"Great, Sarah will cook anything you want."

"Okay, know what I thought?"

"No."

"Let's go right to Edward's new house and see if we can catch a few of those black mussels. Then when the fishermen come in at Bartlett's Landing we'll see what they've got, and this time I'll do the bargaining."

"Sounds good to me."

He had been with me several times before and liked the "give and take" and hassling we went through with the guys at the landing.

"Shall we go to your house and get some winter clothes and some boots?"

"Nah, if we do we'll miss the guys at 6:00 p.m. Let's go straight to Ed's house," which we did.

He had on a $1,000.00 Singapore suit, new black tassel loafers, a silk Singapore tie and a raincoat, no hat. I was geared for winter and water with an earmuff, hat, heavy quilted jacket, and pants, and good LL Bean boots.

We arrived at Ed's. The dock had not been built yet. We scrambled down the embankment in the dark onto the gravel beach, cold, windy, and wet. "You've got boots on. Step out a little and see what's there. Remember we need to gather in the water or Red Tide might get us."

I went out about three feet off shore in 10" of water. I'm peering into the dark. I think I see some mussels and I yell back to tell him. He, in the meantime, had found an old spade shovel with a broken handle. "Here, I'll throw this out to you and see what you can do."

I muddled around, picked up a couple of mussels, and turned to tell him we needed a flashlight and there he was standing beside me in a foot of water. "Not much luck, huh?"

I started laughing at this crazy friend and said, "Lilly is going to kill you for ruining your shoes, stockings and Singapore suit."

"Forget it. She's not here."

We collected some mussels with our shovel and finally just reached in up to our elbows and collected the rest. We waded out with our treasure. He was soaked. I pointed out sea water was bad enough, but mud was worse and he was covered up to his knees.

"Geez, you're right. I better clean off the mud." He grabbed the shovel, dunked it in the ocean and washed his pants and shoes with salt water until they were clean. I carried the catch up to the truck. He squished along in back. I turned the heater on high. He sat in the passenger seat trying to dry out.

"I think we better go home and get you squared away, don't you?"

"No, no, no. Go to the landing. I'll be fine. What do you think I'm a God damn sissy like those guys in Boston?"

Off we went. I parked at the pier, which was pitch black, and kept the engine running to dry Ned out. Soon we saw the running lights of a small 30' boat. It was the guys I usually dealt with. There were four of them on board. We jumped out and started down the ramp. Ned telling me this time he'd do the talking and show me how.

The boat tied up on the float. We walked down guided by the boat's running lights of red and green. Ned was a weird vision. Seemingly out of his element, but he was having a ball. I recognized two of the men as having worked on the estate during construction. They started to speak but I put my hand up and winked. They knew now who they were dealing with, but didn't let on.

"Hi, fellas!" said Ned in his regular guy tone.

Nobody said a word. They just tipped their heads and went to unloading and about their business ignoring this well dressed stranger on purpose.

"What have ya got tonight?"

"Scallops," was the grunt.

Ned looks at me with a sly grin and says, "How little will you charge me by the pound?"

"Five hundred a pound," was the gruff reply.

"Jesus Christ," says, Ned, "are you crazy?" as he stumbles back.

"Five hundred a pound for you Mr. Johnson, that includes the boat."

"Oh, for Christ's sake," says Ned, "did Dick put you guys up to this?"

We had a good laugh including Ned. They wanted to know if he'd fallen in the ocean.

"Just kidding," says the skipper. "How much do you need?"

"How much a pound?" says Ned.

"For you Mr. Johnson they're free."

"Great," says Ned, "I'll take two hundred pounds."

They laughed and gave us ten pounds of the finest freshest scallops in the world. This led to a bake-off on Friday night with Ned cooking the scallops, and Saturday night with Sarah cooking the scallops at the Pray's Meadow house.

Sunday morning I picked up two Boston Globes. One for me and one I delivered to his house. I left it inside the door believing he was still sleeping. As I started out the driveway, Ned's head appeared out the front door and he yelled, "Tell Sarah she won the bake-off. Next time I won't drink so much wine."

Did we have fun? We did. On Monday, I took him to his plane and noted for the first time a slight reluctance to go back. With shoulders squared, a quick wave, the odd rolling hip walk out to the plane and Ned was gone, back to the battle for the world's money.

CHAPTER 19 – BUDGET AND POWER CONCERNS

I was sitting in the den at Prays Meadow shortly after the Taiwan call looking at cost control records Sarah had been keeping. She had followed the costs of the first phase, which amounted to $9,000,000.00 for three houses; Ned's main house, Edward's house and pier, my quarters at Pray's Meadow, all the landscaping at all three places, the barns and outbuildings.

I had papers on all the tables and spread on the floor as I checked items off for each parcel. It was 8:00 p.m., a normal time for Ned to call and he did.

"Well, hello," he said in his unique tone.

"Oh, hi Ned."

"What'cha up to?"

"I'm sitting here working on cost controls."

"Oh good, let me ask you a question."

"Okay."

"How is the budget going?"

"How's the budget?" I said, "There isn't any."

"What do you mean there isn't any? All Fidelity projects have a budget."

"Yeah, well you had a budget when you started. Now we're a year and a half into the program, we've processed over four hundred and fifty change orders on your house alone, and we're far from done. Hold on one minute and I'll pull the records just on yours."

"Oh, wait a second," he says.

"Wouldn't you like to know what you've spent to date?"

"No! No! I don't want to know."

"Well okay, I won't tell you, but you can't possibly ask me about a budget when I have no control over you, nor do I want any control over you."

"But it's coming out beautiful isn't it?"

"Yes, but there is no budget Ned."

"Don't tell anybody that for Christ's sake," he replied.

"Well would you like to know for example what the dining and living room ceilings are costing?"

"No! No!"

"Alright, Lilly had two small jobs done by Joe Tracy. A couple of tables – would you like me to cost them for you?"

"Dick, I don't care to talk anymore about costs."

Down the line he told me one day there was something else I didn't know about him – the fact he is cheap.

I said, "I know you're cheap. I'm the tip checker when we dine out and you pay."

"Well, I certainly don't over do."

Laughingly I said, "You want all these things, but you haven't got the heart to part with the money. So you're making me spend it indirectly. As you've said before, it's good to have someone to blame. I think I'm the fall guy in this and you'll claim I lost control of the budget."

"Nope, I would never say that."

But, he did.

When we found Edward's house on the water at Bartlett Narrows, we were quoted $695,000 for the two-season house and 300 lineal feet on the ocean, plus eight acres. I thought it was an excellent buy and we bought in on a Wednesday night in November. Two parties were flying in on Saturday and we didn't want to lose it, so we closed right there. Sarah put down the earnest money. The whole property was bought sight unseen by the Johnson's.

The next day I went over to walk the lot lines and the acreage. The map of the waterfront had been marked as 300 feet plus or minus. I had a 100 feet tape with me, found both sideline markers and measured out to 400 feet plus or minus. That's a serious difference when waterfront was going for $2,000 per front feet. I kept quiet, not my problem.

Shortly after the paperwork was completed and we owned the place our electrical contractor, an island native walked up to me and said "You know Dick, the previous owner, laughed all the way to the bank on Edward's deal."

I took the heat. We'd been good to this guy and we didn't need the rumor around the island that we were sucked in by the natives.

I said, "Look, we've been pretty good to you. Your first bid on the lake job was so low I didn't think you were going to finish. We've fed you guys more changes, legitimate of course, than you've ever seen in your career and you've recovered, right?"

"Yes, I have."

"Now, it seems you're going around town telling people Dick Larson is a horses' ass for buying Edward's house."

"Well, I'm not doing that!"

"I'll tell you something. I stole this from the previous owner and picked his pocket, because he wasn't diligent. I got an $800,000 piece of land for $695,000, plus a house, landscaping, roads, septic tanks, deep wells and electrical in from the street. All free, thank you very much."

"I won't say another word."

"Good because you're either on our side, or you're out period," and I walked off. End of subject.

We had installed near the end of 1997 a lightening protection system on the main house at the pond. I was third on the list behind Dave Blanchard and a carpenter for any type of emergency. Late one afternoon in the middle of a wild windy, rainy thunderstorm I got a call from Boston Fidelity Security that Ned's house had been hit. I rushed over arriving just as Dave Blanchard did. The area near the hot tub took a big whack. You could smell the lightning in the air. The rod system had worked thank goodness. The only thing knocked out were some cabling for the computer system.

This led to several events. One was to do Edward's house, which we later did and the other was a comedic phone call from Ned.

"Dick."

"Yes."

"What would you do if my house caught on fire?"

"I would call the fire department, they would come up and run a thousand feet of hose into the lake, start pumping and put the fire out."

"Dick, don't you know the town of Somesvillle probably doesn't have that much hose. Don't you know that?" he was aggravated.

I said "As a matter of fact I know they do, since they laid them out one day on Northern Neck Hill to drain them, and to make sure they could get to everyone."

"Are you kidding me?"

"No, I was there." I never lied to him.

"Well, I don't like it."

"Okay, what do you want?"

"I want to run new pumps and a fire line system on both sides of the property from the lake to Northern Neck Road."

"Fine."

"That way we will have instant access to valves along the way and we will buy two woven fire hoses with instant connectors. How many feet would we need?"

"Oh about 500 feet in two sections."

"Get 750 feet in three sections."

"Fine."

"That way we can put out our own fires."

"Fine, do you want me to get a price on this work?"

"No! No!" he said, aggravated, "I don't want to know what it costs, just get it done."

"I will do so."

"In fact, we could help put out fires at our neighbors if we wanted to."

"I'm sure they'd appreciate it."

"Well, talk to you later."

"Good-bye."

Now his mind is working overtime and the next day he calls again.

"Dick."

"Yes."

"Let me ask you a question."

"Yes."

"If we lose power in a storm from Bangor Electric, how soon does our new generator kick in?" He was warned about the new fire pump system.

I answered, "So quickly that you wouldn't notice a power drop."

"How come?" he asked.

"Well, we paid about $20,000.00 for the generator, a Cumming Diesel and $5,000.00 for the transfer switch, so we should get that kind of service."

"Are you kidding me?"

"No I am not and never have."

"Are you sure?"

"We test it every Wednesday and it never fails. It gets you right back in power.

This is exactly where he likes to be.

CHAPTER 20 – NEGOTIATIONS

In 1984, the expansion of the company was so rapid they needed more space and fast. They made a deal with the B.R.A. to take over a decrepit building on the Boston waterfront, soon to become the World Trade Center after renovation by Fidelity. They borrowed the money from Mitsubishi as a money partner whose role Ned didn't understand, nor did Mitsu.

Jung Brannen designed the project and an award was made to O'Connell Brothers, who immediately told the architects to get lost, which was not a good sign. In fact, if the project manager for Fidelity had any guts and or brains he would have told the contractor to get lost unless he had been told otherwise.

The project was completed, and lo and behold, thirty million dollars was unaccounted for. No one could find or determine where the money had gone. The cost controls and project bookkeeping was a shambles. Strangely enough, the job came out well. Certainly the bank, which had laid out 100 million as a mortgage knew how much they had loaned, Ned knew he had to pay back a mortgage of 100 million and the contractor had billed and been paid 100 million, *or had he*? In order to have the power to, in effect, fire the architect, the contractor had to have more power behind him than his contract allowed. No one ever figured it out, including an auditor hired late in the eighties to review the entire process. It's history now, filed in the fireplace. Remember Ned Johnson may have been a geek in college, but he was a Greek in business.

During the expansion phase lasting eleven years, three good men were given a shot at second-in-command. Petersen lasted about four years. Lieberman about three, and the best of them, Jim Curvey lasted four. These are all outstanding executives with good track records. All suffered the same puzzling fate. They were rewarded financially, praised by the chairman, the press and Fidelity Newsletter, but shuffled off to what appears at first to be lateral positions, but proved as time went on as demotions, somewhat out to pasture at the zenith of their skills and power.

The question is why? The answer is because they threatened the fragile ego of Ned Johnson; they proved others could do his job as well, if not better than he, and he suffered or imagined he was diminished in stature by them.

The same neurotic behavior displayed in tennis, horseshoes, billiards, or any social game he can't win at. He perceives the person as having wronged him in some manner, cranks up his anger, develops a hatred and has someone else take action because he is too shy to speak or directly deal with the person. The CEO chair is being held for Abbey Johnson who will assume the job when these things happen: Ned retires, a new Peter Lynch is found and third when business picks up and she can become a hero.

A likable Bob Reynolds will be the last before Abby. The only person in Ned's mind who can replace him is and will be Abby, a genetic mirror, and one who has the backing of Lilly Johnson, her mother. Can a young woman with a husband and children run the most powerful financial company in the world, control the directors and operations personnel, keep the skilled and ambitious on board and contained from pushing through or quitting? I don't think so. From one humble observer, myself, and others who currently work with her, there are great doubts.

If nepotism must rule, who in the family could do it? Beth Johnson Ketterson? No. Edward Crosby Johnson 4th? No. Abby's husband Chris McKown? No. But maybe, just maybe, Rob Ketterson could do it; he's at least five years off. Ned can't last that long, everyone has a shelf life and his neurotic treatment of me alone, stupid to say the least, tells me and others his shelf life is about over. At this point in his life, Patty Hurley controls him; she reads things to him (he's dyslexic) and puts whatever spin she wants on the written subject. She interprets for him for her own benefit, and she supposedly as the lawyer she is, counsels him and cleverly leads him down the paths of anger. She's over-stressed and over her head.

For two and a half years Ned and I built one of the finest homes on Mt. Desert Island, through five hundred and thirty eight change orders, about four hundred phone calls and numerous visits by him we didn't have one single argument or disagreement. That time period included finding, buying and renovating Edward's house on Bartlett Narrows, the house I lived in on Prays Meadow and all out buildings and landscaping to the tune of ten million five hundred thousand dollars. There was not one call or letter, or any type of contact to my knowledge from Crosby Advisors until six months after completion and final billing. No contracts, no discussion of rents, no question, nor any visits by anyone from Fidelity. Everything with Ned was done on a handshake or verbal agreement, and we never had a problem.

The Johnson's wishes were met promptly and when they were away, I felt confident enough to make major decisions knowing I could be backed by my friend, which I was. It took three years of political crap, as shown in court papers, a lot of maneuvering and discussion and spying to finally convince my poor friend I was trying to screw him, or whatever. I didn't know a thing about this espionage effort until we subpoenaed all of Crosby's records. I didn't realize I was so important. Why am I in all kinds of conversations and settlement deals about which I hadn't any knowledge? No one spoke to me until shortly before my dismissal when they were sure they had Ned convinced I must go.

This minor skirmish lends itself to the coming issues of nepotism, family dissension, power struggles, bad publicity, and the possible demise of Fidelity's good name and dominance in the fund business. Bob Posen, at one point third in command, discusses the fragility of the companies involved in the market particularity the mutual fund companies, in the Economist Magazine. He is teaching at Harvard; a serious loss of talent at Fidelity.

It doesn't take much. A perception of trouble in management, a scandal of small proportions by a fund manager, impropriety by any of the inner family stockholders, or perhaps another terrorists attack as mentioned by Warren Buffet to alter world markets today.

From my experiences lately with my ex-friend, I'm concerned Fidelity will not survive as the major player without a fresh outlook by the family and the current group of directors, which will include replacing all the Johnson's with a solid team of leaders for the decades ahead.

Ned once told me while we worked on the Maine projects, probably 1996, he would like to see one more generation of Johnson's run the business. I thought at the time he might go public, or sell the company outright and retire to all of his homes, collected furnishings, paintings and I mentioned this plan to him. His answer was "I'm afraid I am addicted to the company forever."

My motivation for everything I did was aimed at Ned – hopefully to entice him into retiring and having some fun with all the stuff we had in Maine, including me. I could see some great boat trips on "Zitan" over to Yarmouth, Nova Scotia up the straits of Belle Isle and Fundy Bay, cruising past big blue ice-bergs – I have seen them by car. I hoped we could have purchased a new "Dehavilland Otter" which seats five and carry a lot of luggage, a float, and land model for Logan Airport, or Long Pond. I had the pilot, John Harkins, picked out, we'd get him instrument rated for flying deep into the Maine woods and lakes. John and I priced airplanes in 1998 for one grand presentation to Ned. I left brochures around the office as a hint.

Finally, I mentioned it directly and included the idea of taking up golf and flying to some of the courses in Nova Scotia and Prince Edward Island, some of which I had played with my brother Fred. I also installed a small putting green and two tees about 135 yards each at Prays Meadow to provide a beginning for him and evening fun when he came for dinner. All my efforts were misconstrued, all my ideas scoffed at, all included as part of my dismissal. What a loss to him of a faithful friend and potential watchdog and companion for the years ahead.

What fun it would have been to be friends and share the aging problems we now face. Why burden Abby, Edward or Beth, or Lilly who have active and longer lives ahead; why not someone your age whose life interests is the same. All that's lost now, lost, I'm afraid, to both of us. I tried to tell him I wanted to remain friends for life, but the way it was set-up by those who preyed on his mind, I simply couldn't afford it.

CHAPTER 21 – BOSTON MEETS MAINE

Island living and island people are different. Not a significant statement as anyone who's done it, or met them can nod wisely. However, until you've spent a significant amount of time with both, you at first think you know, but you don't. It takes at least three years living, and twice that dealing with them to understand what they mean, as opposed to what you think you are conveying to them, and what you mean, otherwise, you're screwed up for the first few years.

Case in point. While the outside of the house on Long pond was being landscaped, the interiors were finished and furniture was pouring up from Boston in guarded trucks, much to the amazement of the natives and me.

The outside designers and interior architects had been working closely with Ned and his personal curators at Fidelity. We, meaning the island crew, and myself were not allowed to touch anything or even look at the covered pieces being off-loaded by the uniformed guards. Jane Johnson (no relation) and Curtis Estes, hired by Ned, supervised the off-loading and placement of each piece like fussy hens.

About 2:00 p.m. in the afternoon in the driveway came a "case in point." Tara Cedarholm, head curator at Fidelity and close confident of the Oracle had driven up from Boston with a heavy, beautifully made, wooden box containing (according to Tara) an irreplaceable work of art – an original large, round, old, Tiffany chandelier. The guards off-loaded the box. Even our carpenters were impressed thinking the box was the art piece.

They placed it on the floor of the hall leading to the down stairway, stepped back as Tara haughtily stepped forward and began to lecture the carpenters and electricians who had been selected to handle the Tiffany. It required twenty minutes of instructions, threats, and warnings of dire consequences to complete what began to deteriorate into a delirious harangue. I had left halfway through to attend to some other problems. Later that day the job foreman called and said she didn't want anyone to even uncrate it until 10:00 a.m. the next day, and here was where the problem started. She would be there to show them how.

I should have picked up the danger signal right at that point. I didn't and it led to a major confrontation of island thinking and a haughty bureaucrat.

The next morning I met in Blue Hill early with the architects planning to arrive at the "great uncrating and hanging" around 10:00 a.m. Tara met me with a firestorm of a tirade. It seems several major things had happened to her. First, at 7:00 a.m. in the morning, two assigned carpenters opened the box, took out the Tiffany, placed it on pillowed tarps looked it over, staged the stairwell, opened the ceiling and built a bracket hanger that would have held a small car. The assigned electrician lifted the Tiffany, handed it to the carpenters who hung it, repaired, and cleaned the ceiling, and the lamp.

The electricians climbed the staging wired the lamp to the pre-wired switches and turned on the lights. All having agreed the job was well done, they cleaned up and walked off to the next project in the kitchen at 8:00 a.m.

Tara arrived at 10:00 a.m. and proceeded to the area in question prepared to meet with the men. Of course, she saw, and hopefully understood the lesson the islanders were conveying to her, but she blew her stack anyway and rushed into the master bedroom to find me. I was not there, but two island women were there polishing the Chippendales without having been trained in Boston. She took it upon herself to fire the two women who promptly went out in the yard and started crying. She found me finally, told me what had happened and insisted I fire the crew that perpetrated this crime on her and the lamp. I calmed her down and promised I would chastise the men who did this deed. She insisted I do this in her presence. I asked the men to gather in the kitchen up against the counter. I stood in front of them. Tara behind me with arms folded and eyes blazing, and a crowd of craftsman in back of her in the dining area. They had heard me lecture before and thought I had a fine vocabulary, and didn't intend to miss a moment. I began by telling the guilty four they weren't fooling me. Their actions were a direct refusal to listen to an expert from Boston, and they had put me on the spot as a project manager who had lost control of his men. They shuffled around and looked at each other, I almost broke out laughing. The guys in back did small guffaws of denial knowing I never got mad at anybody, but I always got what I wanted for Ned.

I pointed to each with my index finger and said "bad, bad, bad" "baddest" at Dave Poland the leader. While performing this lecture, I noticed the two women crying in the driveway. During a brief break to let the chastisement sink in I said to Tara, "What happened there?" and she replied, "I fired them." This prompted me to end the lecture quickly and dismiss all of them much to Tara's surprise.

"Tara," I said, "I want to talk to those girls, meet me in the master bedroom in five minutes."

I went out to the girls, they explained, and concerned they would get a bad reputation on the island and never be hired again. I assured them that would not happen. They were to go home for the day and be back in the morning for new assignments; also, Tara would be gone.

I headed for the meeting with Tara; she was sitting on the bed seemingly satisfied. "Tara, your first mistake was in not coming to me as the project manager and asking for help. I am glad to cooperate with anyone who comes on the job. These are Ned's orders and I carry them out. Secondly, and I missed this when you told the man you would show them how to hang a light fixture, you challenged them and their skills. I've learned to tell them what to do, not how to do it. They're very proud. The one time I made a mistake telling them, or asking them, if they were going to sweep up on Friday, the foreman came in the office and asked me not to do that again, because the men were going to do it, but didn't like the idea that I didn't think enough of them to have to tell them. I understood and I never did it again, and they never disappointed me. Thirdly, you fired two women who don't work for you. They work for me. You don't fire island people irrationally. It's two small a world and they can't recover."

Tara sat and listened, and to her credit, I believe she understood. I didn't understand where she was coming from in handling all of us like we worked for her, or that her position, especially in Maine, was superior to my mandate from Ned. So I asked her, "Why the disrespect for somebody who has more power than the head of the curatorial staff?"

She answered, "You may have mandates and power," but she said sweetly. "I have mine, too."

I dropped the subject. Tara left the following morning. When we were furnishing the shop apartment building maybe three years later, I asked Ned for help in reaching Tara Cedarholm to begin the process. I said, "Where the hell is Tara? I need furniture and she's not returning my calls."

"Oh," Ned replied in anger, "she's in China peddling her ass somewhere." Once again, I dropped the subject.

CHAPTER 22 – STAR BOARDERS & LOLLIPOP

At Ned's birthday party in Nahant in 1995, we were introduced to Malcolm Rogers. The party was held outdoors at night with candlelights on round tables for one hundred guests. Malcolm sat at our table. He had just been made director of the Museum of Fine Art in Boston. He had been living in England and France and was considered a good catch for the museum. Lilly was instrumental in seeing this happen and was Malcolm's number one patron. During the night, she made several speeches including introducing Malcolm, as well as several other distinguished guests, not me.

The arrangements we found out were for Malcolm to stay with the Johnson's at Charles River Square until he could get his feet on the ground and work into his new position. Now I love my wife and trust her implicitly, however Malcolm was a handsome charming Englishman, cultivated, knowledgeable about art obviously and I wouldn't particularly want him around my house all the time, especially since he's a bachelor. Also, during the evening festivities it was obvious Lilly was quite taken with him.

Malcolm stayed eleven months. Near the end, it became apparent and disturbing to Ned that Malcolm was, or might be the star boarder. We were riding in the truck one spring afternoon in Maine doing our "real guys" tour.

"You know Dick, I am concerned about Lilly."

"Oh, is she not feeling well?"

"No, she's feeling fine. Too fine. I'm wondering if I'm wearing a pair of horns."

"Oh cut it out."

"Malcolm's too content. He doesn't seem to want to leave."

"Why doesn't he get his own place?"

"I don't know."

It turns out all this concern over Malcolm is needless. He finally rents a small apartment in Boston and is joined by the love of his life, a tall, mild, handsome, young man. Mal is gay. Lilly is shocked and admiration turns to anger, which in time gives way to resignation and resumption of what is now just a good friendship. He's a swell guy.

Several years later Mal comes to Maine with his companion. Lilly calls and tells me he's coming, but she would like to set-up sleeping bags for the two of them in the boathouse, so they can have their privacy. I told her there were no toilet facilities, just an outside shower.

"Dick, take care of this please." I dutifully went to town hall and got permission to install an electric toilet, made in Sweden of course. We had it flown over and installed in time for Mal and his good friend.

Lilly once again wanted to know how it worked. I said, "Lilly you don't need to know."

She said, "Dick, I want to know," in tones I knew she wanted to know.

"Well," I said without emotion, "you place a paper liner in the bowl, we've ordered a few hundred, and do your business including toilet paper, stand up and press a button, which dumps the business into a lower chamber, which fries the business into granulated powder."

"And what happens to the powder?"

"We ship it to China for their tomatoes." She cocked her head, looked at me, and closed the kitchen door more firmly than usual.

Ned, not to be left out of the pleasures of life in Maine, decides to get into the act himself.

As he walks around inside his house, he notes there are four or five lovely young nymphs weeding in his garden. Dave Blanchard and I did this on purpose. The thought being the gentler sex would wear well with the Johnson's and their family visitors. Better to have the men in the woods on rough work and the young women puttering around the house grounds.

I noticed when Ned was up alone for periods of time, usually in the morning when things were fresh with dew, one of the wood nymphs would be missing, and one day I asked Dave why she was not working.

"She is," said Dave. "Ned asked her to come in and help polish the Chippendales."

"But we have trained people for that."

"Yes, I know," said Dave, "but he wants what he wants," and with that he shrugged and walked off.

I knew this as "The Chippendale Caper." Few questions were asked; no answers were given, no complaints to me from anyone until we hired a new nymph.

She was a tall American beauty rose, young maybe 19, not married, but had a new little daughter from a high school experience. She had a small apartment in Ellsworth; she had the little girl in daycare. Her parents helped her and I believe the state of Maine. According to those who knew, she did a fine job with the child and loved her dearly. One problem, she had a learning disability, and while working for us on the landscape, she was being set up to train as a nurse's aide in December.

Ned came up alone one weekend in July and evidently spotted Lollipop (her nickname by the crew) working on Saturday in the center of the circular drive plantings. Sure enough, out he comes on Saturday morning to invite Lollipop in for training on the

Chippendales. She didn't do well, she failed in all aspects of the training program.

Ned returned to Boston on Monday morning. Later in the day Dave Blanchard came into the on-site office and told me Patty Hurley, the lawyer, had called from Boston and indicated Ned thought the young lady who failed the training program (he didn't know her name) should be let go because as he said she doesn't have a clue.

I called Ned that night, explained the young girl's circumstances, and asked if he would agree to keep her on until December. I explained we had trained her and she was good at weeding.

He of course agreed. He could sympathize with her because of his dyslexia Lollipop was saved, but I believe the onset of the politics started then. We had refused to cooperate with Patty Hurley and this was noted at Crosby Advisers. We had changed Ned's mind and this did not bode well for the future.

CHAPTER 23 – EATING AND OTHER ECCENTRIC THINGS

At the parties, chefs, bartenders, and waitresses did the work. Lilly, I believe, selected the food menus and Ned did the wines. The guests wore summer informal; nice, but not fancy. The work forces were islanders nicely dressed, not formal. I was always proud of them, especially the young men and women or girls in their teens. They were never nervous, always natural. The guests took a liking to them at the parties I attended.

Ned reminded me when we were together that food and good wine were important to his family and important to him too.

For example, Ned was physically unable to go past the Trenton Bridge Lobster Pound without stopping to eat at any time of day.

He hid this weakness from himself by somehow finding me to blame:

"Dick."

"Yes?"

We should stop at Trenton Bridge for a snack shouldn't we?"

"If you want to," I replied.

"You must be starved?"

"I'm fine. Don't forget you are eating at my house tonight at 7:00 p.m." I answered.

"Well, pull in anyway. I'll buy."

I would pull in at 10:00 a.m., 1:00 p.m., 3:00 p.m., and up to 5:00 p.m. even though we were, this particular time, eating at 7:00 p.m. with Sarah and it was already 5:00 p.m.

I parked the truck. He pulled out his wallet and handed me a crisp twenty-dollar bill. He never carried old money.

"What would you like?"

"I'll have a crab," I said.

"Okay, me too and a diet coke."

I started to the door of the shop.

"Oh Dick," I knew what was coming. It happened every time. "Better get one lobster too, just in case *you're* real hungry."

I went back and got ten dollars more. He's sitting in the truck like a big kid getting his own way.

I came back with the food. I am not the least bit hungry, but those sandwiches are so good. I know I'll eat one with gusto.

We start in with our crab sandwich, chips and our pickle; no conversation, just good eating. We finish about the same time and Ned pipes up "Now, I'll drive while you eat your second sandwich, the lobster."

He goes to get out and shift seats, slowly watching me out of the corner of his eye for my reaction.

"Ned I can't eat another thing."

"You can't?"

"I really can't do it."

He looks at the brown bag puzzled as to what to do, how to solve this dilemma.

"Jesus, I hate to see good food wasted," sounding like the chastisements of my mother regarding the starving Chinese children years ago.

"Well," with an air of complete resignation, "I'll just have to eat it myself. We certainly can't throw it out."

I drive; he eats with his toes curling in satisfaction, I am sure, while I carry great guilt over being such a wastrel.

He loved salmon on the grill. It was one of my specialties at the meadows. I would pick up three pounds on the island. Sarah would marinate the fish for two hours in Italian salad dressing. Ned would arrive on time, usually 7:00 p.m., with the wine. I drank Scotch before dinner and, during cooking, he would help bring things out along with his glass of wine.

He was very consistent when we had him over. He would join me at the grill and say, "What's that you're drinking?"

"J.B. scotch on the rocks."

"You're poisoning yourself."

"It's a great way to go."

"I've got to switch you to wine."

He never failed to lecture me on my foolishness in life of the things that mattered. By this time, he would replenish his libation and switch to landscaping around the house, so as not to be seen by anyone while we were cooking. If I didn't pay attention (I was cooking), he'd stomp his foot and claim he had told me this before and I was not listening. I assured him I was, but didn't want to waste his money (it was his house).

By the time he came back out with his third glass, he switched to outlining a new barn for $500,000.00 that I should do in the backyard. The house was only worth about $450,000. That, I did ignore.

I had put the salmon on the grill with skin down and put the timer on four. He watched intently at four minutes. I turned the fish side down, peeled off the skin and set the timer for three minutes. This seemed to satisfy our normal guests. Not him. He'd lean over and say smugly, "You just ruined some good salmon; you've overcooked it by far."

I took the salmon off when done, put it on a hot plate, and said "Please give this to Sarah while I cook yours." I reached down to the shelf under the grill and pulled out a one-pounder while watching his eyes bug out.

He came back out to supervise. I turned and said "I'll put it on. You tell me when to turn and take-off."

I put it on. He turned the timer to one-minute skin down, turned it when the bell went off and cooked it one minute on the other side.

"Done." he said smugly again.

I said, "It's not cooked."

"All the better," he replied. We ate the marinated; he ate the raw. All had a good evening. As he left to go home, he advised me if I had an upset stomach that night to take baking soda, which seemed to be the best for overcooked food.

When we hiked in the winter mornings, he would invite me in for lunch – an adventure to say the least. He would save food the cooks had made two weeks previous. Ned would never throw out food. We'd take off our jackets and boots and he'd start searching through the refrigerator. Out would come a bowl of something. He smells it, makes a face, and puts it on the counter. After testing a couple of different leftovers he'd say, "Okay, I'll heat this up for you. It's fine with some bread," and he did.

He would make green tea on his power kettle; serve me in the dining room as I read the paper. He came in and set his place up with tea, bread, and the contents of the bowl he'd said was not good.

"Ned, you're not going to eat that?"

"What?"

"That stuff that was in the bowl."

"Of course, there's nothing wrong with it. It's just gone by, but it's good for you."

I lost my appetite, dawdled with the tea and bread and a little of whatever he'd given me. When he was busy reading, I went to the kitchen and dumped the contents. I then surreptitiously walked back to the dining room, patted my inflated belly (a natural condition I'm afraid) and said, "That was great. I'm full and must be on my way."

"Stick around, the cook left some desert I think."

"Oh thanks, but I've got some chores to do. I'll see you tonight."

"Okay."

"Thanks for an enjoyable lunch."

"No problem."

Ned became convinced at one point that sea urchins cured everything. We rode the back roads of Mt. Desert Island constantly stopping at small fishing piers hidden away in the small towns, stopped and spoke to the fishermen.

Sea urchins had no market at the time. When brought up in the nets, they were tossed back. Ned had figured out a way to get them out of their tough round shell. The size of golf balls, he'd eat them raw or with his own invented sauce. I don't know which was worse.

One morning in Bernard, a small island town famous as Julia Child's summer home, we stopped at a small pier, walked down the ramp containing three large plastic drums full of empty crab and lobster shells, and one elderly gray beard fisherman sitting on an empty keg cleaning boiled crab.

Ned had been there before and the old man had promised some sea urchins when his two sons came in with the days catch.

"Well hello."

"Howdy."

"I was here the other day looking for urchins."

"Yep."

"Did you get any for me?"

"Nope."

"What happened?"

"Too busy."

While this extensive conversation was going on, Ned starts picking pieces of empty crab shell out of the big barrels and sucking small bits of meat out.

Ned says, "How much are you getting for hard shell lobsters?"

"Seven bucks a pound."

"I'll pay you that for the sea urchins."

The old man sat back and said, "Mister, I could load you up with urchins all you wanted, but what are you going to do with them?"

"Eat'em," says Ned.

"Well, you'd be a better man then anyone on this island if you can get'em out of the shell; nobody has figured that out yet."

"I have."

"Come back tomorrow afternoon."

We pulled out, Ned had a few pieces of empty crab legs he was working on.

"You've just had your lunch."

"Yep, for nothing."

"Have you figured out how to cook sea urchins?"

"Yep."

"You could create a whole new industry up here. The Japs will buy anything like that."

I swear (this happened in 1996) since then, everyone's trapping urchins using a new method of opening the shell or cooking them, or whatever miraculously came to the island.

As time passed, the eating and cooking became more bizarre at the chairman's house.

Case in point. The Oracle has three microwaves one over the other. He's called the microwave king of the island. If he cooks anything rather then eating raw, which he has now arrived at, he uses the microwave.

One day he comes in with two live lobsters. Turns the micros to 350°, puts a lobster in each, they scramble around until dead at four minutes, out they come and are devoured with great gusto while still green. I fortunately was not at that outing.

By Thanksgiving of 1999, the family all gathered at Long Pond for a four-day weekend. The chef was in the kitchen early preparing a big bird. In walks the chairman, says good morning, and proceeds to take a sharp knife and slice a large piece of raw, uncooked turkey off the bird. Everyone stopped as he again nodded good morning and walked into the dining room chewing with pleasure on the raw turkey meat. Too much!

CHAPTER 24 – CHEAP EATS

In December, 1997 we had wrapped up all the work I had been involved in. We wanted to have David Blanchard, the head caretaker, assume full control of his jobs on both estates, and for Brian LaFauce to take over the punch list from me and begin to work his way in as full-charge project manager.

He was currently functioning as a property manager minus construction in Maine; not as easy as it sounds. Between the four families there are eighteen major homes being used worldwide and a few are company owned, but family used. That's no small task – from light bulbs to light construction.

I suggested one weekend to Ned we sell the house I was using for $450,000, pay back his purchase of $265,000, his construction costs of $50,000, pay me for my furniture $50,000, leaving $85,000 as profit for him. I would go home to Florida.

"I can't stand any more profit. Don't you understand you dope? I'd have to pay bout 90% of that in taxes."

"Well give it to me then. I could use it. I'm not that well off."

"That we could do."

"Okay," I replied.

"Yeah, the problem is I don't want to sell it. Let's keep it and you stick around a couple of years and watch out for my interests."

"I'll agree to that, but I'd like to go to my house in Florida for three months and come back first of April. My project work is done except for the punch list."

"Fine, go have fun. Let Brian clean-up odds and ends and I'll see you in April."

I stopped billing the job immediately indicating to Patty Hurley that we would settle when I came back. I figured he owed me 8% of $5.5 million dollars, which came to $440,000. We ended up in June being paid and agreeing $375,000 was fair and as Ned had instructed Dick Walsh and Patty Hurley, pay enough so as not to lose the friendship.

We came back in April and started landscaping at the house we were living in at Pray's Meadow. I watched out for his interests on all properties and projects without interfering with the management team in place.

Ned and I talked on the phone at night and he suggested I look for property. Edward wanted me to represent the family at the planning board meetings and at the Narrows Associate meetings, which Edward could not face. They were angry with him for putting out the pier and float. I went to six meetings of this irate bunch, and finally one morning a quiet thoughtful neighbor leaned over and whispered in my ear "I'm waiting for you to get tired of this bullshit and blow your stack."

I said, "Never and nothing will ever change." The pier remains.

I got involved in Fort Knox (not the one with the money) in Bucksport, Maine; a beautiful Civil War era construction of granite. Locals were trying to refurbish the building. I thought I could help by raising funds. Ned was willing, but insisted I manage the project and be paid. The locals agreed and we put a request in to Fidelity Foundations for $150,000 to be a matching grant. I put in that budget $40,000 for project management. Two locals took the application to Boston and presented it to Ann Marie Souliere, head of the foundation.

Several weeks later, I got a call from the local secretary in Bucksport. She was excited to tell me they had received the grant. I was pleased, as a historian and Civil War buff; to think of all we could do to bring this fort back. This was just a beginning. I could see bringing back the guns or having exact operating replicas made at a foundry in Ohio. The locals had a plan for using this first batch for re-doing the torpedo house as an educational classroom and tour.

I went out and leased a small car to use on the one-hour trip to the future job site. I made up a budget for requesting future funds from Ned and the state as a matching grant. I needed 130 guns at $11,000 each, plus repairs to the huge Rodman's still there.

I was prepared to ask Ned for $750,000 and the state to match. This would create a truly armed fort and a great educational tool for all of New England and Tourists from everywhere. For once, it would be a project done right for everyone.

Two weeks later the phone rings: "Hello Dick?"

"Yes?"

"This is Christine (the Fort secretary)"

"Hi Christine."

"Well, we just got the money, it's in the bank."

"Swell."

"However, there is good news and bad news."

"Okay."

"Yes, Mr. Johnson approved the gift with the proviso you not be involved."

"Why would he do that?"

"He has big plans for you and doesn't want you tied up for the summer, so we took the management fee out."

"Well, there you are."

"Yep, but we appreciate your efforts, please stay in touch."

I hung up, stuck with a car rental I didn't need, no income, no interesting project and worst of all, no guns.

I called Ned that night and questioned the whole thing. "You were the one who suggested I work and be paid as project manager."

"That's right."

"Why did you do what you did?"

"I didn't, they didn't want you."

"Why not?"

"I suppose they were afraid they'd lose control so they agreed with Ann Marie to knock down the budget by eliminating you and your fee."

"Ned you had control. You could have insisted on my participation."

"Well, let them go off on their own."

"Fine." They spent $200,000 on a new roof for the Fort and never tested it. It leaks like a sieve, which is what happens when local construction crews are not supervised."

We hung up. A golden chance for Maine was lost. What a shame.

I continued to watch out for Ned's interests. I looked at dozens of pieces of property with Janet Moore Real estate. She was favored because she had found Edward's house on the Narrows, a coup d'etat.

One day in the summer of 1998, Ned and I were driving along Somes Sound, the only fjord in North America, to play tennis at the Northeast Tennis Club. Evidently, he could not get in or the membership was full, with some waiting.

"Dick do you have a pedigree?"

"Are you kidding?"

"Well, I don't either."

"Do you think we could have a problem today?" We had been playing for two years as guests.

"I dunno."

"Geez Ned, I don't want to play anyplace I'm not wanted."

"Me neither."

"What shall we do?"

"We could go home and get Lilly. She has a pedigree."

"We'd be late for our match," I said.

"Yeah, let's take a chance."

We walked in through the small clubhouse that let out to a verandah where all the ladies were sitting reading the Wall Street Journal.

Mike Peabody greeted us as any good host would, just as we stepped onto the porch.

He turned to our opponent, his partner who we did not know and said "Walter, this is Dick Larson."

We shook hands, no stir amongst the ladies.

"And this is Ned Johnson."

They shook hands; the ladies lowered their papers and reading glasses and looked to the left in unison, nodded slightly and back to the journal.

Later, when we were dickering for the Farnum Property on Long Pond, I asked Ned what he would do with it.

"You know, it would make a great place for a tennis club."

"Yes it would."

"We could fix up this land with about six or eight courts and have a tennis and beach club on our side of the island."

"I see."

"Then we could send out invitations to all the members of North East."

"That doesn't make sense to me. Why would they apply to our club when they have their own?"

"Not all would apply, but those that do we could reject by sending them a nice letter thanking them for applying, unfortunately you do not have the right pedigree, you simply are not good enough to join our new club."

***

"Hello."

"Well, hello (emphasis on lo)."

"Hi Ned, where are you?"

"I'm stacked up on the ground at Newark Airport."

"Wow, busy huh?"

"Yep, anything doing?"

"Yes, I just completed a tour of the Bangor Waterworks, which is on the river and up for sale by the City."

"What do they want?"

"A dollar."

"Huh?"

"A dollar."

"Grab it."

"Really?"

"Yep, grab it now."

"Okay."

The deal was this. The City would sell the buildings for one dollar, the City would put in $1.2 million, and the new buyer would match that. What would it be? Nobody knew. We hadn't crunched any numbers or done due diligence when Ned said to grab it. I could have legitimately bought the thing since he had told me to do so. I called Brian Reading who was on the committee to sell it for Bangor. He was elated at the news. My mind was working like a trip hammer. I told Brian he and Bill McHenry would do plenty of design work on the project, but I wanted to try to get Frank Gehry in New York for basic concepts of exterior – something spectacular, something to put Bangor on the world map.

A week later Ned called, he began to get cold feet. He wanted Pembroke Company, headed up by Madden and Edward Johnson to meet with the principals meaning the Mayor and the City CEO to review the building and study the feasibility of the project whatever it was going to be.

We hadn't been asked or given a chance to do this because of Ned's phone advice to "grab it" while at the tail of a 737. We had not advised him to buy it; we simply told him about it; he made a snap decision with the comment to me, "Next year's work."

Edward and Madden met the Mayor, reviewed, lunched, and left never to be heard from again until Brian called me and wondered what had happened. What had they thought after three weeks, it was embarrassing.

I advised Brian since he was on the committee to call Edward to find out; also, I suggested if they were not interested that a nice letter to the Mayor declining involvement would be appropriate and good politics.

Brian called; they were not interested and had told Ned it was a terrible business deal. It wasn't our business deal, but we took the hit. Several weeks later Brian got a letter from Pembroke stating no interest, of course the letter should have gone to the Mayor, but Pembroke has the same flaws as Edward does, lack of business knowledge, politically naïve, and lazy. Did they ever really do a diligence report or give another thought to the potential? Dollars to donuts they didn't, Edward just called his father to tell him how dumb we are in Maine, end of project.

I think my reputation as a decent businessman took a hit in Ned's mind. I plead nolo, I didn't advise or consent, but had we bought it, we would have made a success of it because we all loved working for Ned. He engenders strange loyalty from all who work for him. Why? A mystery? No.

His intelligent immaturity, flights of fancy and childish delights at the things people produce, inspire the average person to do his or her best and turns off those who are not interested in anything, or lazy or without creativity or imagination. They are the critics of Ned Johnson. They don't produce, nor do they last long.

***

The summer of 1998 was the first real social season for the Johnson's and the new house. The guest lists were posted in the house and the office. The names I read in the office were paragons of society and finance, the best of the best that come to the island in the summer.

I read the list twice; we were not on it (just kidding) our turn would come. In fact, Lilly called during the week and invited us to Beal's Lobster Pound in Southwest Harbor. We accepted happily and met them at the pier on Tuesday at 6:00 p.m. Ned was slouching along as we went in to order. He wasn't in the best of moods so we all ignored him. We ordered a 1-1/2 pound lobster, one ear of corn, and a dozen steamers for each. Ned stepped to the fore and told the waitress "cook those eight minutes please." She was taken aback as were we. "How do you plan to get the meat out of the shellfish at that rate?" she said.

"We'll take care of that," says Ned. We spoke up. Cook the other three for twenty minutes please," said Lilly.

"You don't know what you're missing."

"Well," says Lilly, "we don't mind missing it. You can tell us about it later."

He paid and grumped his way out to the pier and a corner table. We followed and sat talking to each other leaving him to his dark cloud. I looked around and saw quite a few people drinking wine and beer. I spoke up and said I would go to the window and order some for us.

"You can't buy it here," said Ned. "You have to bring it. Besides you don't need it."

"I know I don't need it, but I would like it," said I.

"Me too," said Lilly. "I'll go up the street and get some."

He grumbled or muttered under his breath about alcoholics. We ignored him.

Lilly came back carrying a cold bottle of white screw-cap wine and half a six-pack of beer. I should have gone with her and chipped in for a full six-pack.

Lilly opened the wine, poured some for Sarah and herself. Ned stuck his plastic cup in front of Lilly. We all feigned surprise. She poured him a full glass. I took one of the beers and we toasted the evening despite Ned being a gloomy Gus. While waiting for the lobsters, we chatted and had a few laughs, Gloomy kept company with himself.

When our number was called, I went up and got the tray. I had to make two trips and wait a bit for drawn butter. When I returned to the table one of the two remaining beers was gone. Oh well I thought, maybe this will brighten him up. We ate lobster, corn, steamers, and Cole slaw; what a feast and he was paying.

In the midst of the hilarity, I reached for my other beer. It was gone. He had it and another full glass of wine. I said nothing, kept eating and enjoying. Lilly spoke up, "Ned for someone who didn't want anything to drink, you have done quite well for yourself."

"Yes," he said, "If you're going out to have a good time, why not enjoy yourself?"

Lilly called again, later that August, "Dick?"

"Hi Lilly!"

"Ned wants to treat the three of us to dinner at the Burning Tree in Otter Creek. They say it's the best on the island."

"That's great. We'd love it."

"How about tomorrow night. We'll pick you up at six thirty. We have reservations for seven."

They did pick us up. We had a two-hour dinner with good wine, good company, but very expensive. Ned got the bill, reviewed it carefully, then he pulled out his wallet and carefully selected two crisp one hundred dollar bills, which he laid on the table and said, "Let's go." I offered on the tip. "No need, all set," he replied.

We followed him out into the parking lot. Lilly turned to me and said in a low voice "Dick go and check the tip." This was not an unusual request. It had happened before. I went back in. The waitress was at the bar cash register. The bartender was taking his apron off. I stepped into the fray. "What was the tip?" The bartender said, "Not enough to have that man back again, which I am about to tell him."

"What was the tip?" I repeated.

"Ten dollars on two hundred," said the waitress. I peeled off thirty more and said, "If he comes in again and I'm not here call this number and it will be taken care of. He is a good guy, but eccentric. I don't want him to have any trouble, He's extremely wealthy – send me the whole bill if necessary, even if it's a thousand."

When I got to the car Lilly whispered, "All set?"

"Yes."

"How much did he leave?"

I lied, "Twenty."

"How much did you add?"

"Twenty."

"He didn't leave enough and you left too much. I'll reimburse you."

"No you won't."

"Dick!"

"No way."

CHAPTER 25 – STRANGE FRIENDSHIP

Shortly after the "Lollipop" episode, Ned arranged to visit for final review of the mechanical systems we had installed in the main house meaning plumbing, heating, electrical and ventilation. They were complicated and difficult when the work was being done because the engineers working with the architect and particularly with Ned had built in redundant systems at his request that would match that of a Boeing 737-A.

During the rough-in stages of the job, and when it was time to start installing the mechanicals, one guy showed up from North East Plumbing and Heating, with frizzy blonde hair, an old, but clean tee-shirt, jeans and flat un-insulated "Larry Bird" type red ball sneakers.

I was standing in the driveway when he pulled in for the first time. "And you are?" I asked.

"I'm John Harkins, the plumber."

"Hello John." I stuck my hand out and shook a medium sized, strong, leathery mitt, little knowing if he was a leading hand, a foreman of a crew, or just a helper driving a truck.

"I assume the rest of your crew is following."

"Oh, not today," he said, "I'm just here to get a handle on the job and start on the layout, and the pipe chases."

"All right, go to it. If you need any help from me, I'll be in the office next to the garage."

John began his work. I didn't butt-in, however, after two weeks I decided it was time for more men from

the plumbing company. I didn't want John to fall behind.
I called the office and spoke to the owner. "Hi, this is
Dick Larson."

"Yes, Dick it's Bob Young."

We had met before during the bid process and
when he picked up his contract after being awarded the
job as low bidder.

"Bob, I think it's time for John to have some help,
don't you?"

"I don't know," he replied, "has he fallen behind?"

It was my custom to have each trade track their
progress, live up to the schedule and be ready for the trade
which had to follow them.

"I don't know, that's not my job, unless you do
fall behind." I said, "Then it is my job."

"Well our position is when the foreman, who is
John, feels he needs help, he will get it when he calls. He
hasn't called."

"Okay," I replied, "I'll check it out." I went to the
site, found John in the basement plugging away and asked
him, "John, how are you doing?"

"Fine."

"Are you ahead or behind?"

"I think I'm running even."

Well, I didn't know it at the time but I had just
met one of the most remarkable men of my life-time.
Flash forward to Ned's visit for final inspection.

"Dick, I've met this guy, what's his name, John, a
number of times over the past two years. I see he's
coming to the review meeting. What does he do? I
thought he was just a worker?"

"Ned, I'll tell you what he does. In fact, it would
be easier to tell you what he doesn't do, but then I
wouldn't have much to say. John Harkins has done by
himself the plumbing, the heating, most of the ventilation,
the wiring of the control systems, the generator piping,
the lawn sprinkler connections, the fire pumps and hose

system throughout the property the boiler room work except for pipe insulation and anything else others couldn't do."

"Jesus Christ." says Ned, "What an interesting guy. I didn't realize."

"I'm not done yet."

"Oh?"

"He is a married man with two nice children and a lovely wife. He is a hermit by nature and can't live near anybody; also, he has to work alone. He is a licensed blaster of ledge, a conservatory trained pianist, the organist at all functions of his church, he built a nice home by himself after work hours, sold it for profit and is now building another one in a remote area. He is a licensed pilot and licensed to handle heavy equipment and trucks, and he owns property in Ellsworth. He has never given me one hard moment. He responds weekends at all hours to my calls for help. He is, to sum it up, a genius and doesn't know it, and he is tireless."

Ned was dumbfounded. I was so proud to tell him about John Harkins. The review went fine. John said nothing unless asked. Ned would look to John, or at him to confirm anything anyone said. John with hands together behind his back would agree with a nod to Ned, or a short answer if something was not duly explained. Each answer was followed by a quick head bow to the great man who would bow back to John. I laughed. If ever, two distinct characters had ever met before, I wouldn't know it, and yet the similarities were startling to me. Here was one guy, John, who really had had no formal education, except the piano and knew everything he needed to know to live and live well by his high standards. Here was the other guy, Ned, who had had all the formal education in the world and learned nothing except what he needed to know to live in his world and live well, and he learned that after school in his own setting, as did John himself. One lived all his life on a natural island the other on an island of his imagination.

CHAPTER 26 – BLOOD BROTHERS

I mentioned earlier that Ned called frequently, probably over four hundred calls in two and a half years. Most were mundane questions about the day's output; some were unique and comedic.

"Hello."

"Well hello."

"Oh, hi Ned."

"What'cha doing?"

"Catching up on the contract forms we're preparing to send out." I replied.

It was early in the job, late 1995.

"Can I help with anything?"

"No, but I do have a small problem you could advise me on."

He wanted to help. It pleased him when I was stuck on something and he could solve it.

"What's that?"

"People who do not know who you are, are asking me what it is you do for work?"

"Okay. What do you tell them?"

"I've been telling them you are a stock salesman in Boston."

"Oh, that is good, very good, very good."

Silence for a good twenty seconds, told me his mind was working, he came back...

"No, no, no," he said slowly, "Tell them I'm a bond salesman."

"Why?"

"Because they make more money."

We hiked a few times out on the ice on Long Pond and to Rum Island and back. Occasionally, we would stop on a cold windy day and shelter in any of the bob-houses, set-up for ice fishing. One day was so cold; we searched a bob-house for anything alcoholic to help get us back. We had to make it under our own steam. It was tough, from that point on I carried a flask of brandy.

Rum Island is so named by Joseph Pulitzer and friends. Pulitzer had a camp on the pond in the twenties and thirties and made his own booze during the depression and prohibition on the island while supporting sobriety in his newspaper.

We frequently hiked on the roads and trails of Ned's property particularly in the winter. One late gray afternoon we were plugging along on his road when he slipped and grabbed the branches of a sharply nettled bush. Blood flowed a little; he looked at his hand and said, "Hey, we ought to become blood brothers."

I said, "Okay."

He said, "You have to cut your finger and then we'll shake."

I said, "I think there's a little more to it than that."

"What's that?"

"We are in the land of the Penobscots, the mighty tribe has rules for all rituals, including the great Penobscot Indian Blood Brother Handshake and Promise."

"Jesus," says Ned.

"Oh yeah, this is not to be taken lightly, you are being watched by the great Sachem in the sky."

"Jesus," says Ned.

"When we shake we have to agree to a solemn promise, that if broken will bring the wrath of the Penobscots down on your head."

"Jesus," says Ned.

"Are you ready?"

"Yes, but what's the promise."

"The promise is I will watch out for you for the rest of your life and you will do the same for me."

"Agreed," he answered heartily.

"We shook and walked off slowly, no doubt in awe of the ancient ceremony we had performed.

I then said to him, "By the way you don't have Aids do you?"

"Jesus Christ no, do you?"

"No!"

* * *

We're walking in Ned's woodlands late one fall afternoon in 1998. Hiking is an art. You move softly through the woods trying to make a small impression in deference to the wood folk who inhabit these wondrous places all their life. You are watchful hoping to catch one of these creatures in a natural mode sharing their lives with you. It's a privilege. Talking with a companion, if you have one, is not good form. You can do that in the civilized world.

Ned's good at it. He's curious, but generally keeps his thoughts to himself. On this hike, I have taken him to an area where I am proposing to build a deer blind for the grandchildren. I call the high area Deer Ridge.

Ned scoffing says, "Why call this Deer Ridge?"

"Because I see a lot of deer here."

"You're kidding me?"

"No, I'm not."

"Dick I've owned this property for a long time and I've never seen a deer."

"That's because when they're out, you're always on the phone."

"Oh bullshit!"

"No, deer shit and you're standing in a pile of it," and he was.

* * *

We're on one of our "real guy" tours in the truck. We're dressed to the nines like down Maine folk. We've even begun to develop an accent, but we only use it in front of each other, otherwise the real, real guys would think we were mocking them.

It's the twilight zone of our friendship. I've finished my work in January of 1998 and have discussed selling Prayer Meadows and going home. His comment at that time was "Stick around awhile and watch out for my interests."

Previously he had indicated he was satisfied with what he had and needed no more property unless something good came up. That's known as a kicker. That leaves a wide gap in his previous statement about enough.

I went to my modest home in Florida for three months, returning in April of 1998 and started looking out for his interests, which were myriad on the island, but required little of my time. I managed however, to review a lot of property from 2000 lineal feet of Long Pond lakefront (for $2,250,000.00) to the Bangor water works building (empty) for $1.00 from the City – dozens of things in between.

One night he called from Boston to discuss plans.

"Dick, I think I have enough property on the island."

"All right."

"Yes, I'm all set, but I want to remind you, you work for me and no one else."

"I understand that."

"Well, I think you should have shown me Edward's place before you showed him."

"But you asked me to look for ocean waterfront for Ed."

"Yes, I know, I know, but frankly if you had shown me first, I would have bought it myself."

"Oh?"

"Yes, I mean what he got was far better than anything I looked at over the years."

"I'm sorry about that. It never dawned on me you would move from the lake."

"I wouldn't have. I would have had both places."

"Well," I replied, "At least it's in the family and with the new pier it gives "Zitan" access to the ocean for the kids and grandchildren."

"That's true, however, anything else that comes up, call me first."

"I certainly will and by the way, there is a home at the end of Northern Neck Road that I couldn't get to this winter because of the mud season, would that be of any interest?"

"No, no. I'm set for now."

We hung up. I sat back and thought of what he had done. He had built a six-and-a-half (soon to be eight-and-a-half) million-dollar estate in the wrong place – a boggy lot on the rocky end of a small land-locked lake. You couldn't even swim comfortably in the place. Camps, not homes, surrounded you. What a mistake! Nostalgia is expensive and foolish.

I did go down to the house at the end of Northern Neck Road. It was beautiful, neat, and commensurate with the area and had fine views of the Twin Mountains.

Several months later, after it had been sold, Ned and I were riding around; he mentioned the house wanting to know what had happened to it.

I said, "It's been sold for $550,000.00."

"Oh, well let's go down and look at it anyway." That was another big mistake.

We did. We trespassed onto the driveway, nobody home, all back in Chicago. We walked to the waterfront.

"Oh my gosh what a view what a wonderful spot, the best on the lake, Jesus Dick."

"I know, I know."

"What did it sell for?"

"$550,000.00." I replied.

"A steal."

"Yep."

"You should have grabbed it."

"But you didn't want anymore property."

"I know, I know, but you should have been more persuasive, damn it!"

"Who bought it?"

"A Chicago banker."

"Offer him $100,000.00 more."

"He won't take it."

"How do you know?"

"Because I came down when they were here, introduced myself, and had a friendly discussion with them about re-sale."

"And what was the verdict?" he asked.

"They said they thought they'd fallen into it and will keep it in the family forever, and told the kids to do the same."

"Damn-it, the trouble with you is you believe everything I tell you, right?"

"That's right."

Later, much to my chagrin, I found out I shouldn't have.

CHAPTER 27 – LOVE REKINDLED

"Hello!"

"Well, hello!" (emphasis on "lo")

"Oh, hi, Ned."

"What'cha doing?"

It's Tuesday about nine o'clock at night in the summer of 1997.

"Oh, I'm just watching the ball game."

"Oh that's nice," says Ned. "I wanted to ask you if the boat house was, or is viable?"

"Viable, for what?"

"For use, for Lilly and me to go in and share a quiet moment together with wine and canapé's or cards, or something like that."

The boathouse was one room of knotty pine supposedly used for storage of sails and oars. Attached to the right was a long narrow room used for Kayak storage and later for an electric toilet. The main room had been restored in the early nineties and had lovely views through two sliding glass doors looking out onto the lake.

"Ned, that room is totally empty."

"Oh gee, that's too bad."

"I'm sorry, I would have got on it had I known you were interested."

I think he was looking to surprise Lilly and put some spark, or make-up, or something into their marriage. We've all done that at times.

We hung up. I sat there for a minute then got up and yelled upstairs. Sarah was reading and said, "Hey come on down and talk. I may have an extra project for us."

I explained the situation, and as usual, she got enthusiastic and said, "Let's do it. Let's furnish it and get it ready for Friday night." We never took the easy way out.

We went to work like the well-oiled team we are. We bought all the furniture from the Bar Harbor Handicapped shop, all the camping supplies at Acadia Sport Shops, rugs, cards, wine from Ned's storage, cribbage board, etc.

We finished the room late afternoon on Friday including two sleeping bags each turned half down. We'd even had a porcelain coated wood stove set on a fireproof tile floor with (thinking sadly of Vitas Geralaitus, the tennis player's death from suffocation on Long Island), fresh air ducting to the chamber as a separate supply from outside.

The room is finished and it's beautiful. You can do anything with plenty of money and good help. Sarah and I were pleased with ourselves and excited about the surprise we'd prepared.

They arrived on Colgan Air Line at the small island airport. I picked them up and dropped them at the house on Long Pond. I gave a hand with the luggage and when Lilly was in the house said to Ned as I was leaving, "Do me a favor."

"Yes."

"Would you go and unlock the boathouse, measure the room and call me right back, the stove man needs the dimensions by 7:00 p.m."

"Sure thing."

"Call me soon."

"Yep."

At 6:30, the phone rang. "Dick?"

"Yes."

"Something's wrong up here."

"Yeah, what?"

"Well are you sure you're keeping an eye on everything that goes on?"

"I'm positive."

"Have you been to the boathouse lately?"

"Yes, I was there today."

"Doing what?"

"Installing your furnishings."

"You son of a bitch. You're pulling my chain."

"How come?"

"This thing, how long has this been done?"

"We finished at 5:30 p.m. today."

"I am pleased, Lilly and I, she hasn't seen it yet. We are going right down, drink that bottle of wine, and play a card game."

"Good. Did you note we turned down the sleeping bags?"

" Good night, Dick."

CHAPTER 28 – MOBY NED

"Hello."

"Well hello,"

"Oh hi Ned, what's up?"

"How about you and me taking Zitan out and heading down to Blue Hill Harbor?"

"I'd love it, when?"

"This afternoon all right?"

"Sure."

"I'll see you at Edward's pier around three o'clock."

"Okay. I'll bring sandwiches."

I headed out at 2:00 p.m. for the Trenton Bridge Lobster Pound, maybe the best in the world. I ordered two lobsters and one crab sandwich with chips. I had a six-pack of beer and some peaches for dessert and headed back onto the island and Ed's pier.

On arrival, I noted a rush of activity as Edward, Allison his fiancée (now wife), and Ned were loading a huge wheel barrel with gear for our trip. I pitched in and helped roll it to the lower raft. Tied up was a sixty-five foot sailboat Ed had chartered.

Ned in the meantime jumped into a rubber dinghy and rowed out into the current and onto Zitan's mooring, which was a helluva long row, but he worked the tide run beautifully and soon arrived and boarded Zitan. Job well done. Problem was he didn't know how to start the boat. Ed and I waited a goodly time, then Ed jumped into a light powered rubber boat, the likes of which most of us have never seen or will own, and flew out to Zitan. This did not bode well for our trip, nor fill me with confidence we could make it. However, I had had a boat in Nahant and felt I would be helpful if Ned needed help.

Zitan was brought in and rafted to the sailboat. We loaded up and pulled out to the cheers and waves of Ed and Allison. Ned was at the helm as we threaded our way down Bartlett Narrows next to the island on the port side. What a day. Clear as a bell; not a cloud in the sky. We cut through those cold Maine waters with the hissing sound of the bow and the rumble of the diesels powering the jet tubes. No old fashioned propellers for us.

We rounded Bartlett's and headed out into the wide bay surrounded by mountains and passing the occasional small deserted island. It just doesn't come any better, the two old guys still had it. Visibility was great, there was plenty of fuel, and seemingly an eternity to live this life and love every moment of it.

The phone rings. By this time, I'm at the helm and Ned is below getting out charts. It's Edward. "How are you two doing?" We had just got underway. "Is my father there?"

"Yes."

"Can I speak with him?"

"Sure."

"Ned, it's Edward." He came up and put the phone on all-call, meaning he was broadcasting to all on board.

"Dad."

"What?"

"Keep those neurons firing!"

"Yeah, yeah, ah Ed, did you fill the fuel tanks?"

"The one you're on is half-full."

"What? What?" Ned asked alarmed.

"The other tank is full."

"Jesus Christ I told you to fill them."

"Dad, you've got enough fuel to go to Boston. I'll sign-off."

Ned starts to flick switches back and forth. I watched the gauges to confirm Ed filled the auxiliary tank. It looked fine to me and I said so.

"Yeah, well you don't know if these switches are right or working, and neither does Edward."

"Ned for Christ's sake, it's fine. Get the charts and let's enjoy the day."

He went below and came back with the charts and wouldn't you know the phone rang again.

"Dad, it's Edward. How are you two doing?"

" Well, we're working on the fuel problem," says Ned.

"There's no problem, Dad."

"Oh yeah, how do you know?"

"Just keep your eyes open for any markers and keep those neurons firing."

I was getting tired of talking about a problem that didn't exist.

Ned picks up the phone and calls Edward and wants him to look up the gas slips so we don't get shorted by some inexperienced fuel guy.

Edward has the slips, calls, reads them over the phone, and repeats the admonition to keep the neurons firing.

By this time, I'm getting aggravated because a good outing is turning bad. With more flicking of switches and more calls (about three more) from Edward, I finally picked up the phone and asked Ed to please stop calling. We are both fine and having a good time.

Ned now has spread the charts and is trying to focus on where we are. Of course, we're heading for the town of Blue Hill, which I can see in the distance and if you look back and follow our wake we line up nicely with Cadillac Mountain, so why charts?

He couldn't read them anyway and I suggested we go by line of sight until we pick up the harbor markers and follow them to safe haven.

He agreed and settled down with some continuing grumbles about Ed and the fuel situation. After sighting some curious black seals coming up to the boat to investigate, he got back into the spirit of the trip and we had a great run to Blue Hill.

Pulling in was a bit much. The markers left us with a choice of two entrances. We chose the port side because large boats, sail, and power were anchored and we thought of deep water. This proved to be wrong and as we watched the Fathometer, we realized we were climbing an underwater ledge. We slowed, stopped and backed out, and headed for the other channel markers. Ned said, "Boy, you are an adventurous guy aren't you?"

I agreed with that assessment. I did take chances, but all calculated from my years of living on the Highlands of Lynn. Take a chance, but make sure you've calculated the odds and they favor you. If you win, fine. If you lose, turn around and try a new tack, which we had done.

We worked our way down the channel passing lovely old Maine homes that had lawns that ran to the water's edge. Ned was taken with an old Inn on the bay called Jon's Inn. The place was for sale. Sarah and I had stopped one day and with the owner's permission looked the property over. We didn't know the asking price. I said, "Ned, that's an old Inn and it's up for sale."

"Grab it," he said.

"What?"

"Grab it, buy it, wouldn't it be fun to run an Inn?"

"Who's going to run it?"

"You are."

"Ha, ha." I laughed.

"Seriously, I'm serious."

"And what would you do other than furnish the money?"

"I'll come up weekends and tend bar."

I tried to gloss over the inn by saying I would look into the finances later in the week.

"Don't forget."

"I won't," and I didn't. We did visit the inn later. Other than being beautiful, it would have been like riding a dead horse, an old saying of my father's when we had an unprofitable job on our hands.

We slid into the dock at the end of the harbor. Ned insisted on docking and tie-up while I acted as first mate. When he felt we were secure, he jumped off the boat and headed up hill to town without a word, head bent on a mission of which I knew nothing, rounded the corner of a boat shed and disappeared.

I wasn't concerned. He was like that in other ways, so focused at times you couldn't talk to him. He wouldn't listen. I settled into a deck chair and started reading the Boston Globe. I had a can of beer, a lobster sandwich, the newspaper and a $500,000 dollar boat surrounding me with all the comfort a Hinckley Picnic boat could provide.

I had a few visitors who came down the ramp to see this luxurious craft. I was pleasant, but let no one come aboard, more or less to curtail any long conversations. After an hour around 5:30 p.m. an old timer came down and said, "Don't want to alarm you, but if you don't pull out in an hour you're here for the night. This channel turns to muck at low tide, which is about 6:30 p.m."

I watched the clock and the lowering water every five minutes, got a little bit anxious and then thought the hell with it if we're stuck, we'll stay at the old inn and Ned can stand for drinks, dinner and rooms since it will be his fault. It's good to have someone to blame!

About 6:10 p.m. a small van rounds the corner, drives down the ramp, stops, and discharges Ned out the side passenger door. He has been antiquing and has bundles of packaged treasures. We load them on, load him, and say good-bye to the lucky merchant and prepare to leave.

"Shall we eat first? I'm famished," says Ned.

I said, "I'll tell you what. I'll take her out while you eat because we have about fifteen minutes to get out of here."

"Why?"

"We're running out of water."

He looked over the side. "Jesus Christ!"

We had about a ten-foot wide two-foot deep channel. A jet boat can do it, but a propeller? No dice.

"Can we make it?"

"I dunno – let's try."

We started up the channel churning up the muck. Folks on boat moorings, sipping Martinis watched two old screwballs trying to cruise out to sea on the mud flats. Zitan was worth the money drawing about 18 inches of water and jet propelled. What a boat. We made it to deep water laughing all the way. Ned ate his sandwich and drank his beer with satisfaction as if he had pulled off a coup in the market.

We cruised for an hour towards Bartletts finally reaching the turning point, which I at the wheel knew was to port and around the short end of the island.

As I began to make the turn, Ned standing against the first mate's chair quietly said, "Your turn is to starboard Dick."

"I think it's to port."

"No Dick, it's to starboard."

I reversed directions as he wished, I knew we could round the Eastern tip of the island and make a longer run to Edward's pier. No problem, but I was puzzled at how easily he lost his sense of direction.

We cruised for ten minutes to the east when he came up to me and in a sad apologetic voice, very low almost whisper, and said, "Dick, I'm sorry. You were right, I was wrong. We need to go back."

"Oh, it's no problem Ned, we can round the far end of this wide channel and approach Ed's from the other side."

"No, no, we must go back the way we came."

By his tone, I knew he was embarrassed, and I turned and headed in the direction he requested. We were quiet. I was sad. From start to finish, the trip pointed out to me things were not getting better. Ed knew, Allison knew, and I knew, and I believe Ned knew his time, like the tide – was running out. Ned is a gallant fighter though, like nobody I ever knew, or probably ever will.

CHAPTER 29 – TOURS

As the house neared completion inside, I began to receive requests by phone from the wealthy part-time summer residents. The line ran they were good friends of the Johnson's and they were sure they wouldn't mind if we showed them the inside of the house.

My answer was always the same. You can review the landscaping and I'll be happy to provide a gardener to conduct the tour. However, if you want to see the inside, please call the Johnson's and have them call me. That usually took care of phone requests. They really wanted to see the interior and most didn't call Lilly or Ned.

I didn't take or conduct the outside viewers, but occasionally Ned or Lilly would call and give permission to let friends see the interior. I did all of that because there was so much to see and explain plus the breakables were precious. Those who knew what they were looking at went through quietly and thoughtfully, and I followed answering the occasional intelligent questions. Ned had asked for a temple quality building. He got it and you can feel it as you walk around. The house is not church-like, just a quiet reverence for life, good living, and good craftsmanship.

Then we had the other side from Johnson friends who weren't knowledgeable or appreciative of what they were looking at. That tour went something like this:

"Dick, I love that chest."

"Yes. It's 400 years old."

"Is it Chinese?"

"Yes."

"Oh Charlie, come look at this chest."

Charley comes over, looks, and says, "What about it?"

"Doesn't it look exactly like the one your uncle's second wife had in Newark?"

"It does, but hers is more shiny and the hardware on hers is better."

"Yes," she replied. "And not loose."

I gave them one more chance by showing them the Chippendale chests in the bedroom, but I didn't have much hope.

"Dick, what nice bureaus."

"Yes."

"And there's three of them."

"Yes."

"May I open a drawer?"

"Yes, I'll help."

"Oh," she looked in. "The bottom of the drawers are so old looking and notice how cracked the wood is. That should be repaired."

End of tour.

We had a lot of that. It's a form of one-upmanship used on all occasions by some people. It's hard to do with Hepplewhite, Chippendale, Tiffany's or a magnificent Fitzhugh Lane, but lots of people try with self satisfaction because they don't know what they're talking about or looking at.

The third type of viewer is easy to handle. They go through both levels. I say nothing unless questioned. They take about 30 minutes and when done and saying good-byes out in the driveway, the woman leans to convey a confidentiality to me that always has the same content: "Dick, I like my house much better. It's so homey," and with a kiss on the cheek she blows ten million dollars away, right out the driveway. All of our work is gone for the sake of hominess.

Ned came alone one weekend. He was tired and needed to be left alone to do nothing, and he was. I dropped the Sunday Globe off at ten in the morning. He came to the door in pajamas and invited me in for coffee. I said no thanks politely and as I turned to leave he said, "Do you know what I did yesterday?"

"What?"

"Nothing."

"Good, keep doing it."

I pulled away in the car, but noticed three empty cardboard boxes on the side deck. He had bought something and I was curious.

I waited until he flew out on Monday and went back to the house as I always did mainly to see the housekeepers were working. This time I wanted to see what he had bought.

In the living room, he had installed a new stereo system with speakers and a mass of spaghetti wiring. When he wants music, he wants it. I would have the electrician do some clean-up work. The system, which I immediately played, was magnificent and filled the living room with vibrant sound. What make? Bang Olefson made in Sweden by little trolls or something. *Wow*, I thought, as delusions of grandeur flashed across my brain, *I must somehow get one of these systems.*

Several months later, I was in Naples, Florida for a breather. Sarah wanted to shop at the Waterside Shops on the North Tamiami Trail and I went along. While wandering around on my own, I spotted a Bang Olefson store and went in. At the side wall, beautifully displayed with other sets was Ned's stereo system.

There was no price tag of course. This was a class operation. The salesperson came over and asked if I needed help.

"Hi," I said, "I 'm just browsing."

"Fine if I can help, let me know."

"Thank you."

I wandered around nonchalantly then turned back to the system and asked politely across the room, "How much is this system?"

"Four thousand dollars plus tax."

"Oh," I replied.

"How about these telephones?"

"One hundred dollars plus tax."

"I think I'll have this white one."

"Very good sir."

When I left with my phone, I thought they must sell thousands of these phones under the same circumstances. A clever sales ploy to dig a hundred bucks out a poor slob like me. I still have my phone and I like it. It sits silent on my night table in my Florida home in the over fifty-five park.

One afternoon a car with Florida plates came along the main driveway. I was standing at what we called the "crossroads," if you went left you would arrive at the guest cottage and the generator complex. If you turned right, you would come to the circular driveway and the main house. This car turned towards the main house. I stepped out and held-up my hand, he stopped and opened the drivers side window.

"I've heard there's a house for sale in here."

"No, you're in the wrong place sir."

"I see. Is this new construction?"

"Yes it is, but not for sale."

"Well now, sir,"

I'm dressed in Chino's, an old shirt, and sneakers and he's lowering himself to call me sir.

"I sell real estate in Florida, and one thing I've learned in life is everything has its selling price."

"Well sir," I said, "you're in the wrong neighborhood."

He was getting ready to get out of the car and argue when his wife said, "Come on, let's go."

If he had gotten out and was wearing light plaid blue pants, a white belt, white shoes and Aqua Velva shave lotion and said either "by cracky" or "by God," I would have firmly requested he leave. He didn't get out. I directed him around the circular drive to exit, and as he went by, I spoke in her window, "I'll bet your name is Gladys and his is Clyde."

They continued out with a wave. I wasn't feeling so hot that day, so I left and went for a swim.

On rare occasions, one of the craftsmen whom we employed would show-up with his wife and children. I gave them the full tour inside and out and never failed to point out sections of the building the father and husband had worked on. Sunday was usually the day this happened, right after church and Sunday school. The kids were well dressed and behaved, and I loved the little families that came to see and take pride in the work Dad does during the week.

Occasionally, I had to go to their houses on a business mission. The modest homes were sweet, simple furnishings fresh and airy, but lived in freely by everybody. It makes for a warm welcome for visitors and for kids coming home from school or play. The yard had stuff, all kinds for the kids and the father to play with from swings and balls to junk trucks or parts of boats, but that is rural Maine. Maybe there is something to this homey stuff. Surprisingly, Ned and Lilly's house has great warmth and comfort. With a little push, he could become a "down-Mainer." Lilly wouldn't make it – too much Boston rub-off.

CHAPTER 30 – THE CRITIC RETURNS & COFFEE TIME

The social season of 1998 began and ended in August, the only month the Johnson's spend at Long Pond, other than a few weekends during the year.

Edward and Allison have the same schedule at Bartlett Narrows usually arriving at the controversial pier in a huge chartered sailboat, sometimes with several couples their age. Edward is an expert sailor. I sometimes thought anybody who could handle a boat that big must have had a pretty good brain in his head – an unused resource for his father.

Ned continued to bring small interesting artifacts he had collected, usually in China. The house began to take on a flavor of the Ming Dynastic ruling house of the late period meaning to me about 1600 or later. Lilly had drawn a line in the sand about where that influence would come to a halt. It appears to have been the library, leaving Ned the living room and dining area to create his own museum. It all works. We've got Ming, Chippendale, Bermuda, Hepplewhite, Colonial, The Jazz age (1930's), pool room blah, Modern America and bland.

The season of 1998 was not the best. The house was not quite up to par. Lilly had been busy and other than coming to our place, or having some friends including us over, I don't recall anything special. Ned and I did our thing together. They sailed and boated with Edward and his fiancée. I think Lilly was bored until Abbey and Chris came with Julia, the new grandchild.

The most exciting event was Ned in the middle of the lake, falling out of the kayak and not being able to get back in. Later we went to the sports store and bought a device to assist re-boarding. I became concerned for everyone's safety on the kayaks, so I bought a used rubber dinghy and a small 7-1/2 h.p. motor and left it hooked up at the kayak float. Ned scoffed at the thing telling me I was a worrywart. He refused to pay for it.

One Saturday afternoon I got a call.

"Hello Dick, hello Dick, this is Zitan calling, answer. Come in please."

"Hi Ned. It's Dick. Dick!"

"We're at the entrance to the Mud River," he says. (In the background, Edward is saying loudly. "Dad, don't call Dick.") Edward's getting sick of me because his father has faith in me and likes me, and Edward is concerned. I mentioned this to Ned once and he replied Ed was very protective of his mother and father. He wanted their undivided attention.

We had looked at property that month on the river in Lamoine and Ned had decided to investigate by water. The river is tidal and you have to watch the tide charts.

"Dick, we are stuck in mud."

"No kidding?"

"Yep."

"Okay why are you calling me?" I asked.

"Just to let you know we're stuck."

"Okay, what can I do?"

"Nothing, I just wanted you to know."

"Has Edward got the answer?" I asked.

"He's going to reverse engines."

"Sounds good to me."

"Yep."

"If that doesn't work you could get out of the boat, you and Ed, stand in the mud, and push it out."

Edward came on, "Dick we're all set, we'll be fine."

"I know, Edward, I know."

"He grabs the phone anytime there's a problem and calls you or me."

"I understand Ed."

We hung up. All I could think of was Humphrey Bogart pushing the "African Queen" with leaches all over his body. If that happens to Ned, he'll sell the boat.

The season ended in late August. The Johnson's left; the tourists left; and the islanders, including Sarah and me, settled down to the rhythm of fall foliage in October. The first frost and snow arrived in late November and after Christmas in Massachusetts with our family; we left for Naples, Florida for four months.

Ned and I talked occasionally on the phone. I still had and do have now an avid interest in all the properties we had developed.

One night he called to tell me about a meeting he had just left at 9:00 p.m. at his private dining room. He was enthusiastic about the President of Deutch Bank and his second-in-command.

"I tell you, Dick, this guy really impressed me as a powerful executive."

"Really?"

"Yep, Gary Burkhead came by my office around 6:30 p.m. and told me he had a meeting set for drinks and dinner in the private dining room, would I like to join in?"

"Did you know who was to be there as guests?"

"No, but when he told me I said absolutely I would like to meet this famous guy."

"And how did it go?" I asked.

"Fabulous, I was fascinated by this guy's brain, he was brilliant."

"Wow!"

"Yep, when we took a break I asked Gary in our private men's room why this guy is coming to see me?"

Gary said, "He owes you three billion dollars."

"Jesus Christ," I said, "If I owed anyone that much money I'd go see them every week."

Sarah and I returned to the Island in April. I had landscaping to do at Prays Meadow and to honor my promise to watch out for his interests.

Lilly had begun early in the 1999 season to plan for August in Maine. Obviously she had put more time in for the coming season, it was great.

The gardeners had the place looking like a million, check that, five and a half million. Lilly had gotten an invitation in the mail from David Rockefeller for a garden tour in late June. Ned came up with tickets for Sarah, me, Ned, and my daughter Nancy, who took Lilly's place. She had been enough times.

While driving up to the garden tour, Ned reminded me to remind him about being critical of things. We parked and walked through the oriental wall that surrounds this wonderful magical place. The Chinese theme was reinforced throughout – ancient prayer gongs, statues, flowing water around oriental stones all surrounded by flowers and shrubs indigenous to Maine's climate.

Ned takes Nancy by the arm. I follow, he leads us to an ancient Buddha, "See this is nice, but it doesn't belong here. It should go over there."

I said, "Ned, don't forget."

"What?"

"Your promise."

"I was just mentioning to Nancy this might go better over there. Just a comment."

We moved on.

He kept a watchful eye out for me through the rest of the tour. Commenting to Sarah or Nancy slyly, I gave up and said nothing more. On the way home he commented he didn't care for flowers.

"Why not?" asked Nancy?

"Because they look too sweet, too much like candy or frosting." He preferred shrubs and rocks, and things.

"Plus, I only come up in August when everything has stopped blooming."

* * *

It's a cool Saturday morning on Mt. Desert Island, crystal clear with a blue sky and a deeper blue lake at Ned's house. I'm there to have coffee with them, just the three of us at Lilly's invitation.

Ned is sitting at the dining room table with his breakfast bowl piled high with fruit, slurping up health, of course.

"Dick, I'll make some coffee for all of us," says Lilly.

"Fine." Since I'm invited for coffee, it would be nice to have some.

Lilly, who can't cook or won't cook, is going to show Ned and me she can make coffee in the coffee maker just like that.

I'm facing the kitchen, reading a section of the paper, since Ned doesn't like to talk when he's eating. I can't see the coffee maker because the folding doors are partially closed, but it's close-by.

Lilly says, "Coffee's on guys. It will be ready soon. I'll be right back." She heads for the inner chambers. As I read, I hear something dripping. Thinking it's just the coffee pot, I ignore it until running across the counter and down the cabinet face is dark brown liquid coffee onto the floor. I bury my face in the paper. Ned is focused on his bowl as Lilly comes back in. Nothing is said. She closes the door firmly and obviously cleans up the mess with towels. She forgot to put the pot under the brewing spout. Poor Lilly, she screwed up making coffee. Even I can make coffee.

About ten minutes later, she opens the door partially and says, "It will be ready shortly. Is there anything I can make for you guys to go with the coffee?"

"No, no," I said. "I've already eaten my breakfast. I'm full."

"How about you Ned? Eggs, bacon or toast, or all three?"

"No, no, I'm full."

She knew all that. She was trying to redeem herself in her own eyes. I couldn't help but laugh, but not out loud.

"Coffee's ready. Come and get it."

I got up, went to the kitchen, reached into the upper cabinet, and took out a cup. Cups from cabinets in Maine are cold. I like to pre-heat mine so the coffee stays hot longer after pouring.

I'm standing at the sink filling my cup with hot water. A small face appears at my shoulder with an attitude. "Is there something wrong with that cup?" Lilly demands standing with her hands on her hips.

"Oh no, no Lilly. I'm pre-heating it as I always do in Maine."

"Oh," she says calming down.

"I always do that too," says Ned.

"Ned, I've never seen you do that."

"Lilly, I probably do it when you're not around." he replies.

"Oh bull. You just said that to help Dick out."

"I don't think I'm in trouble," I said.

"You're not," she replied. "But you could have been. By the way, I have a bone to pick with you."

She's feisty now and wants to argue, which is a natural mode with her. She is very nice, but a bit eccentric and acidic in her general conversation and puts one on the defensive quickly.

"Dick, every time Ned and I go out to visit the neighbors here on Northern Neck Road, or along the pond we end up talking about you and Sarah, and how nice you are for most of the visit, and it's getting to be a bit much."

"It is a bit much," Ned mumbles with a mouth full of fruit.

"Why is that?" says Lilly.

"Yeah, why is that?" mumbles Ned.

Now I'm on the spot. I'm up to my ass in trouble. I have to respond and defend myself. I never expected to be attacked like that. I just came for coffee.

"Well, Lilly," I sigh as I think like a bugger. "I'll tell you why. You see, you and Ned are a very famous couple and when you show up at people's houses they get very nervous."

"Oh cut it out. We're just folks." says Lilly.

"No, Lilly, no, no. You are not just folks. That's what you like to think. You'd like to go back to the good old days when you came here to camp in your father-in-law's place, which was a wreck. You are the most powerful financial couple and family in the world.

"Oh, cut that out," she replied heatedly.

"Lilly, Lilly," stutters Ned, "we probably are. Dick may be right."

I'm getting mad now with their antics, plus I've come up with a good answer. I lean forward towards her to emphasize my explanation, "When you visit, people are so nervous they reach for some common ground in which to conduct a conversation with these famous drop-ins. Sarah and I are that common ground and that's the thing, the only thing they can come up with to not feel like their making fools of themselves."

She started to interrupt me. I cut her off. "And when we go and visit the neighbors and friends as you do, and we've been here five years, and they know us better then they know you, all they talk to us about is you and Ned."

"There isn't anything I can do about that." I said. We're famous because we're friends with you two. We're infected; we've got the Johnson fame virus. We can't be cured unless we leave the island."

For once, Lilly was speechless and the Mumbler couldn't even mumble. That problem was solved and the solution was the right one.

CHAPTER 31 – POOR LILLIE

Lilly is not a people person. She tries to be kind and thoughtful, and succeeds to a degree, but she struggles within herself to overcome or push back against Ned – a powerful, overwhelming personality unless he pretends to kow-tow to her or some other member of the family. Over the years of putting up with his eccentricities she has lost her own persona and tries to regain it in a strained manner consisting of a defensive posture that breaks down under any change that strains her pre-planned course. She has a hard time with adversity and has great difficulty dealing with illness or poor health, or old age, even within her own family or relatives.

Case in point; Ned's cousin Joan Fisher owns beautiful oceanfront property on the quiet side of the island. Joan is a world-class numismatist, very pretty, 62-year old woman, never married to my knowledge and a hermit living a life that excludes personal contact as much as humanly possible.

Ned loves her dearly, which I believe is enough to turn Lilly off. Joan lives in upper New York State and comes to an ancient cottage in Maine for maybe two months of the year.

Joan came down with breast cancer in the late nineties and was treated in New York. She came to the island in 1998 for her convalescence. We made her acquaintance at a clam dinner Ned put on at the guest cottage with Sarah, Joan, Ned and I. Lilly was in Boston.

Joan and Sarah hit it off and later in the week, Joan called Sarah for some help in procuring groceries and going with her to visit a doctor for a check-up, including staying with her throughout the procedure.

Sarah worked with her during that summer, and unbelievably, was allowed into the kitchen several times.

Joan and Sarah usually communicated by phone or if Sarah had to bring something over, Joan would leave a note halfway up the driveway on a bush telling her where to leave whatever it was, usually near a rock halfway up. Sarah would leave her note on the package or a bush.

The next year she came to the island and was not well at all. Ned found out what Sarah was doing and went on one of the trips to the hospital sitting in back with a dear friend of ours who had come up to visit. He lectured our friend in whispered tones she should inform Sarah of anything needed, regardless of expense, Sarah was to do for his cousin.

All was done, but Joan had a relapse and went back to New York. Ned soon forgot about Joan, sadly enough, but Sarah did not and they frequently talked over the next few months on the phone until Sarah left the island forever under duress. Where, one might ask, was Lilly during Joan's visits and illness? Frankly, I don't think she cared for Joan. I think it irked her that Joan was there and was ill to boot. She had, from what I could observe during my work, washed her hands of the whole thing and didn't care to think about it, and probably never had or did.

I believe she has administered some of the charitable giving by the Johnson Foundation, and for this she and Ned are to be commended, of course. In Ned's case, he has been heavily involved in solving the Alzheimer's disease with enormous gifts of money and a personal presence in the laboratory he has founded and supports. Of course, the solution would be a magnificent gift to the country and the world; if our roles were reversed, his comments would be that what I gave was self-serving, since he has become mean-spirited, but I won't say that about him.

Lilly does not have a good reputation as a caring person. She seems to turn-off sick or elderly people. She seems to ignore the inevitable situation we all will find ourselves in; all the money in the world can't replace sincere, loving care.

Parties with wonderful guest lists posted a Who's Who of American Finance and Socialites from the island, plus the whole Johnson clan. All came off to perfection, at least the ones we were invited to attend. There were glitches of course, several comedic, most just fine. I liked the odd happenstances and I like to write about them as fond memories, not to be critical.

We were partying away one night, about ten couples in the living room – guests were being served great finger food as appetizers, the bar was sending out martini's, manhattans, white and red wine, beer or anything the guests wanted. I wandered into my kitchen (I mean their kitchen) to apprise myself of the operation. Two chefs were in control with two young island girls as waitresses and one young woman as bartender. All is well. What can go wrong? I meander back to the party; and the doorbell rang. Lilly opened the door. There stood five familiar faces from Nahant, Edie Hunnewell, Hollis Hunnewell, George and Alice Hall, and George's brother, Doctor Hall, a great guy.

Lilly is taken aback. She recovers and invites them in. They take off their sweaters and are introduced to the guests.

I sense tension in Lilly's manner and, sure enough, when she has fully recovered, she walks over to me and says, "Dick, I don't know why they are here, but I don't want them here."

"Lilly, they are your best friends from Nahant."

"I know, but I didn't invite them. I don't know what to do."

"Well, let me wander around and find out what's up."

Ned, of course, is sitting in a far corner of the room with some good-looking woman. He doesn't have a clue, nor will Lilly tell him what's going on.

I walk around. Edie spots the problem and says to me, "what is going on here?"

"I don't know Edie, but it seems Lilly was not expecting your group."

"We were invited to this party on this night. We sailed for days from Boston and are anchored in Somes Sound. This is our party."

"I know, I know. Let me work on this."

"Dick we're invitees. What is wrong with her? She's worse than he is."

I thought about the whole thing and went out to the kitchen. I asked the chef, "We have five more people. Can we feed that many more?"

"Mr. Larson, we have enough food to feed them and the neighbors."

I went back out thinking the problem was solved. Wrong.

I said to Lilly, "Lilly, I just checked with the chef. We've got tons of food."

"Dick you don't understand. I simply don't want them here."

"They think they were invited."

"They were not."

I dealt with the problem directly. What could I do? Ned was not going to help. He was going to be a hindrance. I went to Sarah and said, "You are going home." She put her glass down. God love her and said, "Okay, to do what?"

"To prepare dinner for seven people including you and me."

"What am I going to serve?"

"I'm going to bring the Nahant folks over. You have everything you need except the main course, which will be eight one and one-half pound lobsters cooked and cracked at Able's Pound where I will pick them up.

She quietly left. No argument, no questions and went home to start. No wonder I love her so much after fifty years together.

I turned back to the room, went to Edie and said, "There has been a mistake. There isn't enough food for us. We are going to my house for dinner."

She was pissed to say the least and when Edie Hunnewell of the Wellesley Hunnewells gets pissed, start ducking. She was about to blow, I said, "Edie, we have been friends and tennis partners for years. Do me a favor, gather your group, and follow me, please."

She did it. We had to take Lilly's station wagon, because Sarah had gone in my car to the Meadow.

As we were leaving, Ned leaped up, came to the door, and said, "What the hell's happening?"

I said, "There's been a little mistake in scheduling. We're having dinner at my house."

The irrepressible Edie speaks up, "Nothing wrong with us. It's you."

Ned says, "Dick we've got all kinds of food, what's happening?"

"Ned, leave it alone please."

"Huh?"

"It's been taken care of. Please, Ned, it's settled."

We left as he wandered back to the party without a clue.

We had a great dinner at the Meadows, Dr. Hall claiming he was glad he had come to this party. We all laughed. Edie went with me to help pick up the lobsters after we had delivered the other guests at Prays Meadow; actually, she just wanted to vent and boy did she.

I parked the car behind another and wouldn't you know, the other has to back out while I was in the pound. Edie tried to slide over to the wheel, bumped into the rear mirror, and snapped it off – an expensive repair in the Volvo.

When I came out, she explained what had happened. I said forget it. I'll get it fixed.

Later, we took them back to the dock in Somesville at 11:00 p.m. They had to be rowed individually in a pram out to the boat in the darkness and the murky black water, a nice scene from the 1800's. We yelled good-bye across the sound and went home to clean up the party dishes.

The next day, I returned Lilly's car and explained the accident to the mirror. She looked at me and said, "Did she do it on purpose?"

"Absolutely not." I replied. But, you know, it's dawned on me recently, dumb Swede that I am, that she might have.

CHAPTER 32 – SIMPLY A SHOP AND FLYING

During late August, Ned began to talk about building a shop up in the woods, remote from the main house. I listened as he described a simple building for storage and woodworking. Brian LaFauce, the current project manager, had been in touch with the architects who had sketched what appeared to me to be about $250,000 with a full cellar.

Ned indicated a job start on the first of September when he would go home. We talked about it. He questioned why it was going in the woods. I thought it would be more appropriate in the woods, because it would make faces at the quality of the other new buildings on the estate, but I had not been involved in the process.

The next day after morning tennis, we floated around the new shop area in our tennis clothes. He was disturbed. He was questioning himself. He then answered himself. "I'd like to have this little building placed down in the estate section, what do you think?"

"It would have to be upgraded. Right now, it looks like it was designed by a carpenter."

"You're right."

"It's going to cost you more."

"Yep, but you know we could put a full two bedroom apartment upstairs with a lake view, a great shop with storage and a full wine and storage cellar."

I thought, *Here we go.*

"What do you think?"

"I think you just went from $250,000 to $800,000."

"And we could do decks and a Chinese roof line and do some fancy work inside the apartment; what do you think?"

I think you just broke a $1,000,000." He didn't bat an eyelash. "Would you want to do it?"

"If you're going to spend that kind of money, I certainly would want to do it. You need a full time project manager for that."

"Start September first."

"I'll need a footprint for digging and foundation work the plans can follow, but we've got four months to pour and close in the building. That's a tall order."

"You can do it."

That ended a conversation that led to big trouble and a year later a dissolution of a good solid friendship.

The Johnson family scheduled the leave from the island in late August. They would fly on Colgan Air, which flew twin-engine, two-pilot planes to Boston four times a day round-trip. We had all been flying with Colgan for five or six years. A little bumpy at times, some bad weather, sometimes unable to fly or complete the trip and return to Boston because of fog or heavy snow.

Ned flew up once at night and couldn't land. I was at the airport and heard them, but they went back to Boston and I went home. The phone rang, "Hey Dick, where are you?"

"I'm home, where are you?"

"I'm back in Boston."

"What are you going to do?"

"I'm going to get an ice cream cone."

"What kind?"

"Vanilla."

"Plain or sugar cone?"

"Sugar, I'll come later tonight, it's going to clear. I'll see you at 12:15 p.m.

"Okay."

He landed at 12:15 p.m. People got off, as usual, a bit green. He got off with his usual grin happy as a clam. We got in the truck, he says, "Is it possible we could get a lobster sandwich at Trenton Bridge?"

"Not at 12:30 a.m. at night." That was a major disappointment for Ned.

"Dick?"

"Yes."

"Dave Blanchard."

"Yep."

"The family missed the Colgan Air flight to Boston this morning."

"Oh."

"Ned has hired a charter to take them all back. I've got their luggage in the truck, but I need someone to drive the car. Can you help?"

"Sure." I was puzzled because they had plenty of caretakers to do tasks like that. There was more to it. I didn't question David though. I drove over in my four door Maxima, loaded the people in, and headed for the airport.

I followed Dave's truck through a private gate onto the tarmac where private jets and charters were serviced and loaded. We got out and Dave came over to speak to me.

"Have you seen the plane they're taking?"

"No." I'm looking for a small jet.

"It's over here. I don't like it."

We walked over and there sat a twin engine plane, one pilot and six seats; Ned and Lilly, Abby, Chris and the baby, and a seat each for Beth and her husband Rob Ketterson, now head of Fidelity Capital. My memory of this group may be off, but it held an irreplaceable Fidelity presence.

I didn't like it at all and as an outspoken friend of the family, I had voiced my objections before to Ned. I was told I worried too much, that I was a worrywart.

I went to Ned, "I don't think this is a good idea."

"Why?"

"The heart and soul of Fidelity is in this plane. We don't know who the pilot is or the condition of the plane."

"It'll be fine."

The pilot looked good, clean, white shirt with black tie, a pair of wings on his chest, pressed pants and polished black shoes. He had begun to load the luggage at the rear. The Johnsons piled into the plane and took seats at random. The pilot came from the rear and lectured them all on seat belts and floatation gear as per the FAA if a plane flies over water. I felt a little better.

Ned motioned me to come over to his door, which was still open. I leaned in and he said, "Do me a favor will you?"

"Sure."

"The pilot has gone back to finish loading luggage. Pretend to give him a hand and smell his breath to see if he's been drinking."

Holy shit! I thought, *what a God damn fiasco!!*

I did as asked. Checked the guy out as best I could. He was fine. I mentioned he had a valuable cargo. He smiled and assured me things would be fine. The weather he said is good all the way down the coast.

They took off. Dave looked at me. I looked at Dave. We shrugged and went home.

Later that day about 5:00 p.m. Ned called. "You know what?"

"What?" I replied.

"That was not a good idea. Did you ever think of that?"

"Are you pulling my leg, I have been thinking of nothing else since you took-off. That was wacky."

"I know, I know. Never again."

"I hope not."

"Even I was nervous."

I could only imagine the rest of the Johnson's over Boston and Ned gets nervous.

CHAPTER 33 – HIRED, FIRED AND RE-HIRED

In late August of '99, the Johnson's began to leave the island and return to Boston and the business. Several days before, Ned and I met and made final arrangements for the construction of the shop/apartment building. Plans had to be prepared for his approval later in the fall. In the meantime, the footings, foundations and first floor deck plans had to be on my desk by September 30th to give us the weather we needed in November and December to complete that first phase.

Brian Reading became the lead architect for this job; Bill McHenry would oversee from long range. He was working on a project in Bermuda for Bill Stewart.

I began to line up subs for the excavation, blasting, foundation, and the first floor deck with steel beams. Brian Reading delivered the footprint plans and sketched out the three levels to give Ned and I a chance to study the abstracts. The building certainly had no relationship to the crude drawings done in May.

I also prepared a budget for Ned that started, I believe, at $650,000. After the exterior plans were done, I guesstimated an increase including plain interiors at $865,000. A Ned Johnson barn does not come cheap, too many changes (all for the best) and too complicated.

The surveyors worked with Brian Reading and me to stake out the dimensions. Brian and Ned met with the landscape architect to face the house at the correct angle to the lake and the other houses on the estate.

We had run out of work for Ray Williams, the estate carpenter. I decided since we were obligated to pay him, I would add a simple screened-in porch over at Pray's Meadow. Seven sonotubes, a roof, unfinished walls with screens, a wood floor and minor landscaping, about fifty thousand dollars bringing our expenses on the house to $380,000 selling price when we sold would be $450,000, leaving $70,000 to reimburse Ned and me when I left to go home.

In late September, Patty Hurley from Crosby advisors called me. "Dick?"

"Hi Patty!"

"I just need information for Ned regarding your pay on the new project. What are you expecting?"

"The usual $6,700 per month.

"The same as before?"

"That's right."

Several days later Ned called. I believe on Friday night. "Oh Dick."

"Yes, hi Ned."

"Look, I've been thinking. This isn't that big a project. I think we can handle this through Crosby using Brian LaFauce."

"That's fine with me."

"Yes, he can fly up one day a week and keep things moving. What do you think?"

"What ever you wish."

"I'll be up shortly and get him off on the right foot. You don't have to bother."

We hung up and I said to Sarah, it looks like we'll be going home to Florida, which was fine with her.

Several things disturbed me. I loved working for Ned. I loved construction, but most of all I didn't like what I perceived as some loss of control by he and I with the process. Crosby was becoming a factor in the decision making in Maine, contrary to our discussion in 1995 about full control between he and I.

Since I was now out of the picture, I shrugged off my concerns. When he visited several weeks later, I tried to settle the house issue at Pray's Meadow. "Ned, let's talk about the house I'm in."

"Yes."

"I would like to go back to Florida since I now have nothing to do. Can we sell the property furnished (my furniture), you get all your money back and then some, and I get my furniture money ($50,000) and we're even."

"I'm not sure I want to sell."

"But Ned, it was bought by you to give me a place to live. You don't need it now, nor do I. It took the place of the guest house when you needed it and I had to move."

"Here's what we'll do," he replied. "You stay two more years (definitive) and watch out for my interests."

"If that's what you want." I answered a bit reluctantly.

"Now what's going on at the house you're using?"

"We have no work for the carpenter at the estate or Ed's. You're going to need him in the future and we have to pay him anyway, so why not get something done at the Meadow?"

"Good idea, show me what's going to happen." he asked.

I drew out the simple plan on a piece of plain paper. He studied it for a while, leaned back in his chair and said, "I think you should put a slab in on top of a frost proof foundation, put heat in the slab, you know radiant."

"Ned, you'd have to make this an all season room with insulation, windows, doors, lights, floor tile, and everything needed in Maine weather wise. Also landscaping after the excavation and foundation, it's a much bigger job."

"Let's do it right."

He left. I went to work on the porch revision with

Bill and Brian. You need good architects when you do something big or small. We would have a project to work on; Ray would have something to do for the winter.

We lined up Howdy Goodwin for foundation and Tater Gray for excavation at the meadows. They hustled for me and got it done by mid-October. Ray started; Sarah and I flew to Florida for two weeks. We came back in late October. I was disappointed in Ray's progress, but I chalked it up to bad weather. The process of looking at property for Ned and Edward continued with Janet Moore. I did not visit the new building being constructed at Ned's, not wanting to interfere with Brian LaFauce and Crosby Advisors. I felt politics had played a part in my replacement. The projects over the past three years had turned out well. Projects for the Johnson's are fraught with danger for career bureaucrats, if they don't turn out well. The old saying never rang more true, "Success has a thousand fathers. Failure is an orphan."

As the weeks went by, I became concerned about the porch not moving as well as I had anticipated. I began to think I had made a mistake in trying to use Ray. He seemed lethargic and tired, his hired helper was not reliable, even his wife came and helped; something was wrong.

We knew we had to close in the porch by late December to be able to continue to work inside during the cold months.

Ned had stopped calling me. I called him a couple of times, friendliness was there, but something was lacking.

In late November, he flew up to attend the regular Thursday meeting we had held throughout the projects. Every trade attended if needed, the architects and engineers, and representing the owner, Brian LaFauce who would run the meeting for Ned as I had done.

The rest of the family would come up for Thanksgiving as usual. The meetings started at 10:00 a.m.

and continued until 12:30. When you meet with the chairman on business you must be prepared. You must have an agenda; you must have presentations, physical models, drawings, and verbal discourse. You must be ready to answer dozens of questions about any phase of the project. He is so sharp you must try to control the meeting or he'll eat you alive. You must know when to draw him back from fantasy, displays of creative imagery, and flights of his imagination without hurting his feelings, or losing the thoughts he comes up with, because he may insist you do them.

What kind of management would hire a nice young man with absolutely no training in handling the most stubborn, obstinate, and astute businessman as well as the most powerful financial man in the world is beyond me. There was nothing wrong with Brian LaFauce, there was something wrong with the kind of thinking that went into his selection to deal with a Ned Johnson.

The meeting was a disaster. Ned directed all his questions to the caretaker. Ned doesn't run meetings, they are run for him. He's a counter puncher. He doesn't do agendas or memos, or take notes. They are done for him to read.

The meeting was adjourned; nothing was accomplished. Brian LaFauce, poor guy, sat in a corner frightened to death. He never said a word. To top off the problem nothing had been done in seven weeks on the building. Two months of the best weather down the drain. You can't recover in construction when you blow two months out of the schedule. In the terms of construction lingo that's known as "Amateur Night at the Met," you got a dish each week for two years for perfect attendance, you didn't have to do anything but attend.

The meeting ended at 11:00 a.m. My phone rang at 11:15. An irate chairman was on the line. "Will you please come over here and straighten out this God damn mess?"

"I'd be happy to help out. When do you want me?"

"Right this minute."

I got in my car and rushed over before he got any madder. He was in the yard alone in front of the office. I stepped out and he started. "Look at this fucking mess. Look at it, look at it! Nothing has been done. Am I supposed to do everything myself? Jesus Christ!"

"How can I help?

"Take this job over and get the God damn thing started."

"Ned, I think the problem is I want to be paid for my work." Brian LaFauce was getting $130,000 a year. I was getting $80,000. Something was awry at the business center in Boston.

"Oh, you're always worried about money."

"That's because I don't have any."

"Look Dick here's what I want you to do. Call Patty Hurley and tell her you will do the job Pro Bono. I will take care of you."

"No sir, not me, I'm not going to do that. I have my wife to take care of."

"If anything happens to you, I'll take care of Sarah for life."

"Oh, thank you, but I've been watching out for her for 48 years and I'd like to keep doing it. I'm not working for nothing. I'll help you paint the barn or dig a garden, or whatever, but if I work at my trade I need to be paid just as you do."

"Dick, listen to me. Call Patty and tell her. Trust me. Trust the great Oracle. I will take care of you."

My mind was working like a trip hammer. I thought, why does he want me to do this? Why not just pay me? He must have made a strong statement to Patty about never using me again and didn't want to go back on his tirade. He didn't want to let her see him back down. I believe Ned was trying to save face like Japanese business men; some of whom commit suicide if they fail or are embarrassed. I didn't know. I couldn't figure it out. When the deal came out in court, I was laughed at by our opponents. I still think I was right, dead right, but dead.

I went into the office and called Patty. Ned went with me and said I would do it Pro Bono (big money mistake).

When one of your best friends, who happens to own Fidelity Investments, and makes one million dollars per hour, offers you a handshake and a verbal commitment, you naturally assume this is sufficient to consummate the deal. That kind of thinking was wrong in so many ways. I was never comfortable on the project. Every time we met in Maine or in Boston, I could never again make eye contact with him. He was dodging his own lies; our relationship was never the same. We played tennis, hiked, and worked together, but never the same. He was playing a game with me and I didn't know it. He had reverted to the prep school kids who I knew at Dean. I felt like Ned was being sleazy, acting with no honor, no love, no training, and no knowledge of how to get along with people. I waited until the family returned to Boston, then started the project moving in the right direction.

Again, I state there was nothing wrong with Brian LaFauce. He was just in the wrong place at this time of his career. He was and is honorable, which is very important to the family. He has access to all their homes and children, he's perfect for the job, and he will, I hope, do well. He was run over by a bulldozer of a guy. He shouldn't have been put in that position.

We began the project immediately. LaFauce had lined up the foundation sub, but we put him on hold. We needed to blast and dig a foundation hole in the new location. It was fun to deal with the contractors again. They're shrewd businessmen while appearing to be local yokels. Dick (Tater) Gray was classic.

"Hello Tater."

"Yup."

"Dick Larson."

"Yes Dick."

"How's business?"

"I don't rightly know how I'm gonna get everything done."

This tells the client (me) he is so busy he'd be doing me a favor to come and work, but if he did his price wouldn't be subject to my bargaining. In addition, he's busy because he's good. Everybody likes him and you should too. In fact, it's almost a badge of honor for neighbors to see his trucks and dozers in your yard.

I said bluntly, "I need you on Monday the 2nd."

"I couldn't do it Dick, maybe a week or so from Monday."

That means in (Tater speak) two weeks. "I know you're busy Tater and you have an agenda and I appreciate your honesty. I have an agenda also and yours and mine don't jibe."

"What shall we do?" he asks. Wrong question, but he wants me to make the next move, so he'll know what square he's in.

"Tell you what, Tater, it appears we can't get together this time (I paid him $400,000 prior to this job. I know I have him by the short hairs.). I'll simply have Harold McQuinn come do this one, and when he's done, I'll call you for the next one."

"What day did you say you needed me Dick?"

"December 2nd on Monday."

"What time?"

"7:00 a.m. sharp."

"I'll be there."

"Thanks Tater."

We're into December. Tater is digging and blasting at the shop/apartment. The foundation man has his orders, things are starting to hum, but not at my house.

Ray is dragging and I'm concerned not about costs, but his health.

"Ray, are you feeling all right?"

"No, I'm not."

"You're not yourself."

"No, I've got a big problem. My stomach is all twisted around. I need a major operation."

"Is this life threatening?"

"Yes."

"Do you have insurance?"

"Yes."

"Well why don't you get the thing fixed?"

"I can't afford the weekly pay loss."

"How long to recover?"

"Six to eight weeks."

I called Ned that night. I had taken a chance. I'd told Ray to schedule the operation and not to work until it's done.

"Hey Ned."

"Hey, how are you?"

"Fine."

"What's up?"

"Ray Williams is very sick."

"Geez."

"He needs an operation right now."

"Yeah?"

"He has insurance." I said.

"Why doesn't he do it?"

"He can't stand the six to eight week loss of income."

A puzzled silence hissed over the phone line. Ned just doesn't understand that most people live hand to mouth.

"What shall we do?" he asked.

"Pay him for his time out."

"Geez."

"Six to eight thousand."

"Maybe he could make it up on Saturdays," he says.

"Ned, the quality of mercy is never strained, you've heard that?"

"Of course I have."

"Let's pay him Ned."

"Why don't we give him five?"

"Aw Ned."

"Okay, okay. Tell him to go ahead."

"I already did."

"I know you did; I could tell."

"Thanks, that's a good deed Ned."

"You know me better than I do, but I know you pretty good too."

"You certainly do," I said.

"Good night."

Ray had his operation and came back in four weeks, and up to speed in six, typical Maine worker.

CHAPTER 34 – CHANGING MINDS

We plowed along at Ned's with the excavation – a lot of ledge, a lot of pure clay, and a small amount of water collection in the right hand corner. We sank an 18" diameter shaft outside the footprint maybe 10' away for a pump if needed. In addition, we could measure the buildup if it occurred.

We brought the foundation crew in for waterproof footings, we put a V-groove in the footings poured hot tar sealer in the groove set the forms and poured the foundation on top of the footings and the key.

Brian LaFauce had ordered an expensive water proofing system for the outside walls about $45,000. It was a good idea if we could have installed it in warm weather. We were attempting this in January with temperatures at 15° to 30°; no good. We later used some of the system and returned the rest. The hole was dry. We couldn't see a water buildup, but we coated the lower level and filled all around with a combination of good gravel and stone.

We did not allow the cement to be mixed with an accelerant. We covered all pours done daily with hay and canvas and kept oil burners running through the night in the trenches. Winter conditions prevailed through November, December, and January. It was a tough expensive way to work.

The final building plans arrived from Brian Reading. Of particular interest was a double set of barn doors that would open at the rear driveway allowing trucks and cars to enter. We hadn't planned on this and no matter how many signs you nailed up, someone later on would drive in and crash through into the basement. It might take years to happen, but it would. We beefed up the foundation points, which Brian Reading designed, and we placed heavy steel beams to prevent the potential disaster.

I hired Bond Builders for stock and time installation of the beams, the bar joists and the waterproof plywood deck. This would allow us to put heaters in the basement, help in drying the foundation, melt the frost off the floor gravel and begin radiant heat tubes, wire mesh and the pouring of the basement floor. Also decking with the bar joists and heavy plywood would secure the sidewalls and below grade would prevent the footings from heaving. All was done by the end of January 2000, all credit to our subs. We immediately back filled with good dry gravel, raked it all out, and even laid a two-inch layer of reddish brown mulch raked smooth and contoured. We were set to start up. We looked neat, in good condition and not working in trash, which produces trash. I think all the men came onto the job proud to be part of as much perfection as we could attain. We kept it that way to the end.

Ned didn't call as much as he did on Phase I. When he did or I called him for some item of direction, he didn't seem to have the same interest. I thought he was focused on the money he was going to have to pay me. That might sound self-centered, however, I believe Patty, who, of course, had wanted LaFauce to do the job and couldn't let go, nagged him.

I kept reminding myself it was small potatoes to what went on around the world with Fidelity; however, he has always been a good detail man. Able to switch from big to small, high to low and back, and particularly loves building homes as well as skyscrapers.

He called one night. "Dick."

"Hi Ned."

"I've been thinking about that roof line we're planning to do on the shop."

"Okay."

"Let's think about a hint of up swing on the gables and ending roof lines. A pagoda type thing."

"Okay."

"Have Brian Reading do a mock-up and bring it to Boston. Maybe you could bring it."

"I will have that done."

"Also let's think about Oriental or Far East tints and tones in the guest apartment."

"All right."

"Oh, in the basement, let's plan a nice wine storage area separated from the main room and partition off a section for antiques."

"Sounds good."

"Yep, when can we see some of this?"

"In two weeks. I need to have some things shipped from China, Japan and India."

" Swell, see you later."

" Good-bye."

Strangely enough, with Ned not participating as much, Brian Reading and I had anticipated a design swing in this direction. Brian had gone to San Francisco on vacation and had come back with samples of tile, wallpaper, bamboo flooring, window treatments, tatami mat samples, and some great ideas.

We began a palette of colorful samples from the orient for Ned to select. Brian did a small mock-up of the roof for me to take to Boston.

A week later, I called and got an appointment with Ned to discuss the roof.

I lugged it on the subway, some knowledgeable Orientals smiling, and nodding approval. I arrived at 82 Devonshire on time, met Ned in the private dining room, and set-up the mock-up, which we viewed as we had a nice lunch. Abbey had come through with a guest just before Ned came in.

"Dick, are you meeting with my father?"

"Yes, we're having a business lunch."

"Well we'll slip into this private conference room and meet, don't tell him we're here. He'll come in and take over our meeting," she said laughingly.

Ned and I lunched. I had been promised one hour, when we finished we took the mock-up into his office, set it on the floor laid down on the floor and viewed it from all angles like two kids playing with a toy building. He approved of everything. We then sat and talked. I wanted to leave since I had used up more than the time allotted me.

Finally, Abby knocked, said she had an emergency, and needed him. I left the model and set out for Maine. All decisions on the roof made.

Ned called later in the week and set up a visit to review our plans for the rest of the guest quarters. Our pallets were ready. I had the agenda and the attendees notified. Brian Reading and I would do the presentations. I would chair the meeting from start to finish leaving plenty of time for Ned's frequent questions.

Ned had scheduled Colgan Air for arrival at 5:00 p.m. on Friday on the island. I would be there. They ran into rough weather and had to skip the stop at Rockland, because of too much fog and snow. They circled and landed at Bar Harbor, just under the incoming weather. Everybody got off a little green as usual. The co-pilot and pilot came out last. There was no Ned Johnson. As the pilot, who we all knew, walked past me, I asked him if Mr. Johnson had been on the flight. He replied he had and began to look around the small terminal.

I mentioned I had not seen him get off. The pilot said he had seen him get on.

We walked out in the beginning snowstorm, climbed the small ladder stair, and looked in the plane. There at the back in the end seat was the great oracle studying his laptop. He looked up.

"Dick," Ned said surprised. "What the hell are you doing in Rockland?"

"I'm not in Rockland and neither are you."

The pilot and I laughed. Ned started laughing as he walked down the aisle.

"What happened?"

The pilot answered, "We skipped Rockland because of bad weather."

"Geez," says Ned. "I thought the flight was nice and smooth."

"You, Mr. Johnson, are our best customer. You never complain."

Riding home in the truck, Ned says to me, "It wasn't that good a flight. I had a guy sitting next to me telling me all about the stock market for one hour. If he'd only known whom he was talking to he would have shut up."

I started laughing and said, "But you don't know anything about the market do you?"

"No, and neither does anyone else, including the guy on the plane."

We had our meeting at 10:00 a.m. the next day. I usually opened with what the guys called, "Random Thoughts." I then would do a round robin of responses to my thoughts and complaints with tradesmen, giving them an opportunity to defend themselves. Ned would sit next to me, asking a question on occasion. Brian Reading then presented the color charts and palettes to Ned. The meeting lasted two hours, all aimed at the chairman.

In this, and all subsequent meetings with him, I found him to be far less responsive. He was more inclined to just go along with our ideas, in fact, he more than once lost the thread of the conversation and had to be brought back into the meeting by me. He made very few contributions. He even made several phone calls while we talked. I was surprised, concerned, and disappointed.

This was not the Ned Johnson who had worked in harmony with me from July of 1995 to January 1998. This was another Ned Johnson who came to us in January, 2000; not the same guy.

After the meeting, several people spoke to me in confidence and thought something was wrong with Ned. He didn't have the old drive or interest. He wasn't feisty. I covered by saying he was tired and strained (and he looked it), and had too many things on his mind other than our little project. I spoke to Brian Reading later in the day and advised him from my point of view he and I would be making most of the design decisions from this day on, or we'd never finish the job. Brian replied making decisions made him nervous, especially with Ned.

"Then I'll make them, and keep you off the hook," and I did.

Strange things began to happen other than the odd eating habits. He became critical of the estate. We'd hike and he'd lay out big programs of things to do or criticize certain people who had responsibilities and say we'd better fire this one or that one. I tried to explain the ramifications of that particular action and he'd always respond with "I guess you're right."

"I'll do whatever you want."

"No, no, you're right."

"Shall I leave it in place?"

"Yes."

I didn't care if I was right or wrong. I did care about him not being happy about anything. We were all trying to please him.

My daughter, Nancy, came to the island for a few days and drove over to say hello to Ned. He and I were sitting in the office talking. He saw her coming down the path and became alarmed, "Who's this?" he asked anxiously.

I turned, looked, and said, "It's my daughter, Nancy."

We stood up when she came in. He gave her a kiss on the cheek, sat down, turned on his desktop computer with his back to us, and proceeded to punch keys. Nancy looked at me after a couple of minutes completely puzzled. Ned had known her for twenty-five years. He had seen her several times socially on the island. I shrugged and made gestures for her to leave. She said good-bye to us and started out. He jumped up and said to me, "Come on let's give Nancy the grand tour."

She pleasantly declined and left.

Later in the day, I met Nancy at the Meadow house. She was a little disappointed at the reception, but most of all at his appearance. He looked seedy and strained, and was trying hard to act normal she commented. I told her, "He is getting older, and more eccentric, just forget it."

The job progressed through the spring of 2000. The roof was being worked on. It added about $150,000.00 to the budget and was worth every penny. We had ten roofers on it for about six weeks working seven days a week.

The building was, like all buildings, at a slightly dangerous stage whereby visitors to the job site were advised not to enter or climb ladders or staging, and temporary railings were inviting. We kept a close watch on the situation. Still, on weekends, I would go over and find a couple or an old timer (probably younger than me) inside or on the staging looking out at the lake or something. Ned had called during the week indicating he would be up at 10:00 a.m. Saturday to see the progress. I cautioned all the workmen on site to keep an eye on him and if he wanted to do something foolish or dangerous to try to stop him or if they couldn't stop him, assist him to try and keep him safe.

I got to the site the day of his arrival at 9:00 a.m., my usual office time. As I rounded the circular driveway, I noted a crowd on the roof, which was 50' high and sharply pitched and peaked. There sitting at the very top with a shit-eating grin was the chairman. He had arrived early. One-upsmanship was his game. I got out of the car, he waived nonchalantly, "I hope you fall on your butt," I yelled up at him; everyone laughed. I climbed up to the second floor staging, the men formed a circle around him, two holding on to Ned and brought him down safely. He was empowered now and wanted to walk the staging around the house with me.

It was safe. The men had put up temporary railings just for this occasion. We looked at the framing that was still exposed under the shingled dormers.

"Dick, look at some of these mitered joints. They're not as good as the old Chinese building built 400 years ago."

"No, they're not, but we call this rough framing. It's solid as a rock and well done."

"Are you satisfied with this?"

"Yes. If we framed like the old Chinese, this building would cost $40,000,000 too. That ended the complaint.

Ned began a campaign of complaints about the landscape architect who he himself had contracted with before my being hired back in November 1999. Karen Kettlety was a nice person. Ned complained she did too little for her high billings. When I came back to work this was a constant source of irritation to him. I purposely began to work with her to find out what the problem was. I would call; she would come over and discuss the program and the costs anticipated. I would study her plans after she had left and I frankly couldn't justify her whole billing. The problem was that since Ned had hired her, she worked for Crosby Advisors. She billed and was paid by them. What business did I have butting in on Crosby? On the other hand, I was supposed to be in full charge.

Ned called. "Dick, how are you?"

"Fine."

"Dick, we have to do something about Karen. The bills keep coming and I can't stand it any longer."

" Why doesn't Crosby fire her?"

" Dick, do me a favor. Have her send her bills to you. Crosby can't handle this," he said with a touch of impatience in his voice. "You look them over. If they're okay, have them paid; if not, fire her."

I called Karen and requested her presence at a meeting in my office the next day. She came into my office with a wry grin on her face. I faced a hard job. I began a speech I had prepared. She stopped me and said, "Dick, I know why I'm here."

"You do?"

"Yes and you're perfectly justified in what you are going to do."

"Karen I appreciate you're making it easy for me. You know I'm going to let you go?"

"Yes, I do."

"You simply are too expensive and the performance isn't there."

"I know, I know."

"What's happened?"

"I got in over my head, hired some help that hasn't worked out too well, and I really don't know what to do with this project. I'm so concerned about the whole thing that I'm relieved I'm being relieved."

We laughed.

I said, "What does the future hold for you?"

"I'm going to Cambridge, Massachusetts and become an acupuncturist."

She did.

A couple of days later Tater Gray dropped into the office with his consistently high bill and plopped it on my desk.

"You know, I met Karen Kettlety several weeks ago, and she told me you were back in charge, and I said to her, 'Karen, you have met your match.'"

"I have?" she asked.

"Yep, you will not survive Dick Larson because you don't and you won't understand him."

"Is he difficult?"

"Not at all. He talks nice and calm, but if you listen to him, you realize he's asking for super performance. If you don't deliver the goods, you're gonzo."

"I'm not that bad," I said.

"Oh yeah, well I just found out she's gonzo."

Karen had designed some expensive work around the new building. Anticipating the foundation would be exposed she had specified Deer Isle Granite to clad the cement exposure. We ended up with a three-inch problem, which we ignored. The savings was $55,000.00. There were all kinds of shrubs, stones and plantings, paths and bridges. We eliminated most of it and saved $85,000.00.

We also eliminated a large amount of landscaping around the existing main house she and Ned had discussed and saved another $80,000. The total amount saved was $220,000.00. I put in ten months before he fired me at a cost to him of $67,000.00 (which I never got). Near the end, they, meaning Ned and Crosby never acknowledged any savings of which there were more, but harped on my pay, or insisted on rent payments for a house I had been promised as part of the original package. It was all politics; all a great big red herring.

I believe I called Patty Hurley in January and asked for something on account. I was polite, quiet, and not forceful. I simply asked if something could be paid on account. Later in depositions and in court these requests were characterized as harsh and demanding.

Why did I make such a request when I had said I would do this job pro-bono? It was simple; I was losing faith in Ned and his promises. After one of our meetings when Ned was there and we were alone I said, "Are things going to your satisfaction?"

"Yes they are, much better."

"Ned is there any reason I can't be paid something on account at this time?" (maybe April)

"Well, what is it you want? Do you want a loan?"

"No, I don't want a loan. I want whatever it is I've earned."

"Well, maybe I should just give you a million dollars and all your worries will go away."

"I just want what's due under your promise to take care of me."

"I'll talk with Patty."

Several days later Patty called and indicated they had worked something out. I was to receive $6,700 per month less $1,300.00 per month for Pray's Meadow, and less $700.00 per month for an apartment in Melrose, which I used maybe ten nights per year, usually on his business. That is $8,400.00 for ten nights in an apartment, or $840.00 per night. Wow. Plus, the $15,600.00 per year for a house I was told to stay in and watch out for his interests. "To hell with it!" was my mental response. "No thanks," was the verbal response. I didn't know which way to turn. Patty didn't know. I'm sure, he had promised to take care of the money situation when I had told her I would do it free.

Ned and I continued to communicate although far less frequently than before. In 50 years of contracting, I had always finished a job I had started. I had done literally thousands of contracts. Some contracts were written, some were handshakes but I had never been taken or put in the position I now found myself in.

I sat in the office one morning thinking of the project. I could see I would be responsible for landscape design and installation, interior design and installation, and all furniture, window treatments, bedspreads and so on. Of course, I'd need professional help, but I was responsible, the person who got things done. I decided to let out the plumbing, electrical and mechanical to Bond for two reasons. First, there was a shortage of skilled men on the island and we, meaning Ned and I, had no leverage left for future work.

Bond on the other hand did six houses a year and could bring a lot more pressure on subs than we could with probably our last major effort on the island. Having Bond schedule these trades, including bids, would free me up to tackle the previously mentioned tasks. I hoped to complete the project by the end of December 2000, or January 2001. My budget was going to balloon to $1,200,000. The job eventually finished in July 2001 without me and without landscaping and cost $2,200,000. I sent a letter to Ned and some family members after the trial just to remind them Ned had been criminally assaulted in his pocketbook, a high cost for small anger, a terrible shellacking for a perceived injustice, a perfect example of "injustice collecting."

The job continued into the summer of 2001. I tried not to lose my enthusiasm. What man, however, especially a workingman, can be happy doing his trade and not be paid? While his customer or employer makes a million dollars an hour. That is difficult to swallow.

At one of my meetings in Boston, an associate told me in confidence Ned doubles his investments every year. I thought it a preposterous statement, but who am I?

In all the years I worked in Maine, I never had a visit, to my memory, of any executive from Crosby with one exception. An associate and a technician flew up one day for what I don't know. They went kayaking in the morning and hiking in the afternoon. I thought nothing of it. There wasn't anything they could learn in one day that would do anyone any good.

They evidently thought the same thing. I got a phone call, "Hi Dick, it's Patty Hurley."

"Yes."

"Oh, the technician and I think it wise to make another trip to the island next week."

"Fine."

"He wants to follow-up on some security issues (there weren't any) and I could use more exposure to the Estate and job site."

"Why don't you call Dave Blanchard and arrange for your stay. How long will you be here?"

"We'll do two days and one night."

"Fine, call Dave for arrangements."

"We'll take care of that ourselves."

I said, "There's plenty of room, you know."

"Yes. See you in a week."

The following Monday, Patty called again. Ned had canceled the trip.

Summer came to the island and trouble came with it. The Johnson's came in August for their month. Ned and I played some tennis and met on the job daily. I had slowed down the contractors to give the family a chance to enjoy some quietness. Ned didn't like it. He wanted action and evidently thought I was slowing down, which was not true. I had met with the men regarding giving them some privacy. I had told the foreman that when they left at the end of August, I wanted one crew per floor for four months and drive the program to conclusion.

CHAPTER 35 – A TOUGH MONTH

On August 9th, 2000 I drove to the Melrose Apartment for some business, leaving Sarah at home in Maine. I had dinner that night in Middleton with some friends and got back at 9:30 p.m.

At 6:00 a.m. in the morning, I got a call from Sarah.

"Hi Dick."

I knew something was wrong. "Hi. What's happened?"

"I've had a heart attack."

"Oh no!" I was stunned. She had had a heart attack at 11:00 p.m. the night before, driven herself to the hospital, and was stabilized and comfortable.

"I'm all right. I'm in the hospital in Ellsworth and they've got things under control. They're wonderful here."

"You're sure you're out of danger?"

"Yes, one vein was clogged."

"I'm on my way. I'll see you in five hours." I threw my suitcase in the car. I didn't shower or shave, or bother canceling my appointments. I just took off and exceeded the speed limit all the way to my wife's bedside.

I got to the hospital by 11:00 a.m., found her room, and there she sat drinking a cup of tea. My Sarah, the one person in the world I couldn't do without. I was shaking when I hugged her. I'm not an emotional person, but I couldn't control myself. She calmed me down after a couple of minutes.

"I'll have the nurse come in and explain the situation to you."

The nurse came into the room with a big smile and said, "What do you think about your little wife driving for an hour to the hospital while having a heart attack?"

"I don't think much of it."

"No," the nurse said. "It's not a good idea."

"She's like that. She doesn't want to make a fuss or bother anyone," I said.

"That's what 911 is for. That's why we're here Sarah."

"I know," said Sarah. "I know. I just didn't think it was that bad."

It was a clogged vessel, and later on August 15 she had a stint put in at E.M.M.C. hospital. The operation proved successful.

Frankly, I felt guilty about bringing her to Maine for 5 ½ years when I had promised her only one year. Most women would not have put up with the pressure of dealing with Lilly, Ned, and the family for that length of time. She stayed without complaint knowing I enjoyed the work. The insecurity, the eccentrics, the dysfunctional behavior of the Johnson's was undeniable. One never knew what was next, especially from Ned during the latter years. The family would not oppose his decisions on anything, nor confront his anger. One day we were friends, the next who knew?

I visited Sarah every day in Ellsworth and in Bangor, returned to the job site each day, and on occasion knowing she was safe and stable, played some tennis with Ned at Northeast.

We got along pretty good socially and on the job site. I was invited by Lilly to dinner with Allison's father and mother. They were lovely people. We all got on well. The date was around August 13th I believe. I assumed Lilly was aware I was without my chief cook and helper who was preparing for her heart operation in Bangor, hence the invitation. However, dark clouds were rising in Ned's mind and at Crosby. I could sense the animosity in him and them.

Ned and I were invited to play tennis on Saturday the 20th by our friend Mike Peabody at Northeast. Rob Ketterson, Beth's husband, made up a fourth and he and Ned played Mike and I. We had a damn good match, but unknown to me I had been fired on August 18th by Ned and Crosby Advisors. I was not only a lame duck I was a dead duck, but nobody had told me. Gutless.

On Sunday the 21st, Ned got two sets of the Boston Globe, one for me, one for him. I dropped by to pick mine up. Ned came out and threw the paper in one lump into my stomach. I caught it and looked up surprised and startled by his manner. He said nothing, nor did I. I drove off.

Later in the day, he called and asked me if I wanted to play at Northeast on Monday the 22nd with Mike and a friend. I agreed. The invitation made me feel a little better.

I picked him up at 8:30 a.m. He came out, looked at my clean car and started kissing the front fender, muttering nice car, nice car. Can I explain what that was all about? No. We drove off down Sergeants Drive along the Somes Sound passing pleasant, light conversation.

We played Mike and a friend named Clem McGillicuddy. We mixed up the doubles playing with different partners each set. Clem and I finally teamed up together on set number two. During the play, I hit a ball at Ned that went through his legs. We all laughed except Ned. He looked at me and said, "You just made me look bad."

I was puzzled. I had never heard that from him before.

Clem and I walked back to our positions, Clem said to me, "Is he kidding?"

"I hope so," I replied.

"I don't know about that," said Clem.

Later he hit me on purpose. I didn't care, but I told him we're even now.

Earlier that day when we were leaving to play, Lilly had asked me to get Ned home by 12:00 p.m.. They had a sailing date he had missed before because of not getting home on time. I kept watching the clock while Ned and Clem talked after the match. Finally, I got up from the verandah and said, "Hey Ned, we've got to go."

"Jesus Christ, don't you know I like to talk once in a while?" he responded in anger.

"That's fine by me, but Lilly wanted you to make the sailing time today."

He calmed down, "Oh, oh, that's right."

We started home. He starts to tell me about a dinner he had attended at Don Pierce's house on the island.

"Dick, he must have spent two or three million dollars. It's not bad, but it can't compare to the warmth and craftsmanship of our house. I told Lilly, we owe Dick for this, I don't know what I would do without you."

I said, "Well geez Ned, since you feel so complimentary today, could I prevail upon you to make some kind of payment on account?" That only made matters worse, though I didn't know it.

He said nothing. We rode along through a heavy woodsy section near Somesville. He was just looking out the window then he spoke, "You know, someday they'll find me wandering around those woods, lost with no clothes on."

"Aw cut that out, you're fine." He had said things like that to me and I always responded in a positive manner.

I dropped him at home. We always enjoyed the tennis and both said so. His comment, "That was fun."

"It was and thanks." I drove off. Those were the last civil words we have had since.

I went home and did some chores, and an hour later Patty Hurley called and said, "Dick, I've sent you a fax to the office."

"All right."

"You may want to go over and get it, but I'll tell you the essentials."

"Okay."

"Mr. Johnson does not want to deal with you any longer. You are off the job. You must vacate the house. NO money for your furniture and no pay."

"Really?"

"Yes."

"Well I'm sorry to hear that. I'm confused. I'll get the fax and respond. Good-bye."

I went to the office and got the fax. It said essentially, what she had said on the phone. When I got home, Lilly was visiting with Sarah who was convalescing from the operation. I said, "Lilly, I think Ned and I are going to clash."

"No you're not."

"I'm afraid so."

"It's not going to happen." She left. Putting on the best face I could, I brought Sarah up to date fearing her emotions would precipitate a setback of her health.

The demand for vacating was harsh. There was not enough time to sell off the furniture and clean up our business on the island. Included was an offer to pay us $30,000.00 provided we would sign a confidentiality agreement, but no payment until we were out of the house. In other words, they didn't trust me after six years.

A second offering of $50,000.00 including extra time to leave followed up that offer. In addition, it stated Mr. Johnson appreciated my efforts on the projects and my contribution artistically on his behalf (or words to that effect), but he felt it best we now go our separate ways.

The relationship was no longer viable (meaning profitable to him) or words to that effect.

I felt he'd gone around the bend. I called Lilly for help. She said she could not help and hoped it wouldn't ruin our family friendship.

I called Edward and explained the situation for fifteen minutes hoping he would assume some responsibilities for his father, help ameliorate a bad situation turning worse. He could not help. He didn't want to get involved.

I sent two letters of conciliation to Ned. Nothing happened.

I delivered all records to the office. On driving out, he was standing in the woods next to the driveway. He wouldn't look and wouldn't speak. My work was over, as was the friendship.

I had spent forty years in the plumbing business, the last ten chasing money every day. I was tough and an expert. I had to be. My payroll was $400,000 weekly. I decided on one more ploy I had used in years past. A blunt attack on the psyche of the client who wasn't paying his bill.

I called Ned. "Hello," he answered.

"Where is my money?" (The emphasis on money.)

"What? What?" he stuttered?

"I want my money!" I repeated.

"You, you'll get your money."

I hung up. I never got my money.

I sat down with Sarah and outlined a game plan to send boxes to Florida. I would send her to Florida and I would stay behind, sell off the furniture, and get some help boxing our belongings. She flew home to get out of the line of fire. I sold off everything at a loss, and then called a good legal firm. I met with them and they took the case, then I went home. The end of a large piece of our lives, the end of a bad situation getting steadily worse, a bum deal from a wealthy guy.

We were deeply depressed. I, more so than Sarah, thank God. I came down with prostate cancer a year later, high blood sugar, and high cholesterol.

Depression shuts down your immune system. Am I blaming anyone but myself? Absolutely not. I had dealt early in life with emotionally deprived kids in prep school. I knew when I went to Maine what I was dealing with. I shouldn't have taken on this neurotic savant.

Lilly had said to me at his birthday party in 1995 in Nahant, "Dick, are you going to take the construction on in Maine?"

"Yes, I am."

"He will drive you crazy."

"Nah, I'll drive him crazy."

She was 100% right.

CHAPTERS 36 – HERE COME THE LAWYERS

I had hired Rudman and Winchell from Bangor to pursue my claims. The lead lawyer was Attorney Frank McGuire, the lead litigator was Attorney John McCarthy. I met with them in October of 2000, laid out the situation. Frank took voluminous notes and we met several times. I was very satisfied with my team and am to this day. Frank had cautioned me regarding my usual optimistic behavior. The comment that sticks with me was "there's an awful lot of zeros in back of his name. Doesn't that bother you?"

"No," I responded. "Not in America." He smiled sympathetically at my obvious naiveté. In fifty years I had never been in court except as a Juror. We met again in December. I flew up from Florida, strategized for a few days, and flew home for Christmas.

The first six months of 2001 were very depressing for Sarah and me. What a loss – furniture, a home, money I had hoped to earn over the next few years. Six years wasted late in our lives, six years of accomplishments negated in one day. What I thought was a solid, fine friendship turned to distress and hatred.

We needed to begin bringing ourselves back, physically and mentally. We started a program of swimming, bicycling, walking nature trails, good reading, eating healthy food, and trying to rid our minds of this disaster. Let the lawyers handle it.

I found this hard to do as did Sarah. In fact, we couldn't do it. It was time for a physical for us both. We scheduled appointments at the Cleveland Clinic in Naples. Sarah passed with flying colors. I did not. While driving to Maine for the depositions in July, I called the clinic for the results of my tests. Diabetes had come on, high cholesterol had come on and the detection of prostate cancer. Wow! What a surprise. If I wanted to live, I needed some radical treatment. The physician at the clinic calmed me down, told me I had time to make sensible decisions and we would proceed when I returned from Maine.

I was deposed on July 16, 2001. I had no problems with the process. I told the truth of course, without hesitation or qualification. Ned did not attend that day. Patty Hurley did.

Patty was deposed on July 17. There were no surprises. It was quite straight forward, thought I was guilty of indiscretion, really had no grasp of the Maine project. She only knew what Ned had told her or what we had talked about in several meetings and on the phone.

I thought my deposition and Patty's a boring waste of time, but necessary. However, I think we all felt this thing would settle out of court for a reasonable sum. We were all hoping Ned wouldn't come to the deposition. We hoped he would call it all off, pay what he owed and continue his very busy life. I couldn't see him spending more than an hour on this minor issue, never mind the publicity it would generate. I felt he was in a lose-lose situation. It wasn't worth his effort.

But no, he had more to prove in his mind and ego than the rest of us. He showed on July 18th for his deposition. It was a long difficult process as Atty. McCarthy states on page 129 after hours of questions to Ned. "You are the most difficult person to get a simple yes out of I have ever met."

I sat and listened far into the evening and later re-read his statements as printed. It was the biggest bunch of baloney. Totally misconceived or non-informed at what took place in Maine for five and one half years. He either was sincerely misinformed by his staff or made up answers as he went along. He couldn't give a straight answer. I was amazed at what I heard. The truth is simple most of the time; it's yes or no. Occasionally, one can't recall or remember, that's fine and acceptable. When someone is constantly stalling or hiding behind comments like: "I can't remember - I believe - I'm not sure - I don't recall - I don't know - I don't believe," then you know he doesn't know much about things he's trying to talk about. On his deposition he answered questions using the above phrases 344 times compared to my answer to the same number of questions – 12 times.

Ned appointed me to conduct his business in Maine with a simple handshake and a verbal agreement. Then he came against his friend (me) with a complement of people who didn't know anything about the whole situation. In addition, he didn't know, forgot, or ignored the simple fact and totality of the work I had completed on his behalf.

Ned owns Fidelity. If you can't trust him, all other investors and the country itself are in trouble. I am in trouble. I took Ned at his word. I was told by higher authority in Fidelity to get things in writing if Ned made promises. I met a Senior Vice-president one day on Congress Street in Boston. He stopped me and said, "Dick, I know Ned Johnson is a personal friend of yours, but I'm telling you he's a nut." I laughed. "We should all be so nutty."

Now, after the deposition, the thought occurred to me if he wasn't a nut in 1994, he was certainly gaining on it. Here's a guy who in the year 2000, the year in question, made conservatively one million ($1,000,000.00) per hour (forty hour week, of course) fighting his friend for a couple of hundred thousand dollars for twelve minutes of his income. Just the risk of the whole thing puzzles me, and must have puzzled his family and officers of his company. In 2000, the company after paying all overhead, all bonuses, all officers including the family members who work for Fidelity, including Ned, made a net profit after taxes of $2.2 billion dollars ($2,200,000,000.00). The family shares allowed them to take half ($1,100,000,000.00) plus their own investments, which Patty Hurley told me at a meeting in her conference room that Ned doubles his investments yearly, which amounts to another $1,000,000,000.00. That's how you make $1,000,000.00 dollars per hour.

Does anyone in the world know more about Ned Johnson, the Maine projects and Dick Larson than Ned and I? No, so why or where did all these experts come from. They don't have a clue.

One guy showed up as an expert witness for the Johnson group regarding real estate rental on Mt. Desert Island. He was going to testify in court and explain how much rent I should have paid if I hadn't had a verbal agreement in 1995 to not pay rent.

He came up with a gross rental income due Ned on the Pray's Meadow house for four years of $116,200.00 or $2,420.00 per month.

The Crosby group, at Ned's instruction, then determined I should be charged for an apartment at Fidelity's Pine Bank Complex (50 units) I used about ten nights a year mostly on his business.

All that adds up to $3,260.00 per month for 48 months, or $156,000.00 for rent owed to Ned by me while I was on assignment in Maine for the four years, I didn't or couldn't stay at the guest cottage *as promised*.

At court, the Judge dismissed the expert. The whole business was a hypothetical waste of everybody's time, all done on conjecture that went back six years. Politicians at Crosby who convinced Ned I should be fired, yet couldn't come up with reasons, invented all of this. They played on his mind; the "injustice collector" took the hook and ran with it. Half the stuff, half the letters or notes of conciliation by me were read to him and misconstrued if they were read to him at all, which I doubt.

Back in Florida, we continued to work on health and money issues. How were we going to survive on the social security income, a small pension, and some interest on a few thousand dollars invested in Fidelity? We had lost almost $100,000.00 of our cash in expenses, furniture and car rentals in Maine, plus loss of potential income from the construction of the last building, maybe fifteen months up to $101,000.00, which he refused to pay.

Health was first on the list. Sarah loves Florida and she does and did just fine on her heart problem. I was told diet and exercise was key to diabetes and high cholesterol. I implemented both and beat the two problems in six months. Cancer was something else. You're helpless without good doctors and the correct procedures.

I had good advice from my original prostate checker, Doctor Morse at Salem Hospital in Massachusetts. He checked on cancer units in Florida and set me up for treatments once we had decided what to do. There were four choices. One – do nothing and keep checking it, two – have the prostate removed, three – radiate it 18 times and have seeds implanted, or have 43 radiation treatments and try to kill it. I chose the last – 43 treatments five days a week for about nine weeks. I signed up for fall of 2001. I was told I might not feel so good for that period of time plus a few weeks after so I decided to see how tough I was and signed up for real estate classes at the same time. The course was for nine days, nine hours a day and a two-day prep for the state exam.

I started both programs despite Sarah's protests. I figured I could only feel so bad, pain comes in one place at a time. I hated study, always did, so I figured what the hell, give it a shot. I was in an inordinate amount of pain and misery. I damn near didn't make it. I was depressed about Maine, the radiation caused nausea, affected my urinating and bowels, and the R. E. course was long and difficult. I had told my instructor I was having radiation early every morning. He thought I was a nut (he was an ex-Marine Drill Sergeant). I probably was at that time.

I hit bottom about the sixth day of both programs. I had to use the toilet every half-hour. He knew and approved of me getting up and leaving for a few minutes without explanation. I got up, went outside, I had discovered a construction port-a-potty across the lawn of the building next door and was using it instead of the toilet in the classroom. There were seventy men and women using one toilet. I was pleased to have found my own personal potty.

I was feeling lousy. I started across the lawn, stepped into a depression caused by a lawn sprinkler, went down like a felled ox, I was sure I had broken my ankle. I limped to the potty on one leg, sat down on the seat to relieve this pressure on my ankle, feeling like ten cents worth of cat food. I looked to the heavens through the plastic roof and said, "Good Lord, what in the name of God did I do to deserve all this at once. Why me? What else can happen? Please can't you help?" It must have been 110° inside the port-a-potty. I rested my elbows on my knees urinated into the portable septic tank and felt my ankle start to burn. I looked down and saw both sneakers covered with fire ants – the kind that bites. I flung open the door in a rage against the world, took my sneakers off, and threw them on to the grass. I stalked in my stocking feet into class (ankle sore not broken). The young woman who sat next to me was alarmed. I soothed her by saying, "If I die in the next few minutes, just call 911 to come and take me away, but please pick up my sneakers on the lawn." She was kind and sat thinking for a moment then said, "What about your new car? (I had a new BMW Coupe at the time). She didn't care about me or my sneakers, she was concerned about the car. My entire persona dissolved. I was a nothing. My real name was BMW Z.3 301 Red Leather Larson. I handed her the keys and indicated if I didn't die, she should return them to me at the end of the day, or call my wife.

They were determined to win at any cost – beat us down and walk away. Someone told me I couldn't win in court because there were too many zeros against us. I didn't believe that would happen in this country. It did. The jury was not our peers. The Judge and the lawyers were in awe of Ned Johnson. The question of truth; the validity of a handshake and promise from a friend was resolved by the Judge and jury as my mistake in having believed him. They said I should not have done so. Shame on me, I had no contract.

I believe in retribution for some crazy universal law or reason. Do something wrong or immoral, it kicks back somehow. I've seen it time and time again, especially when decent people get hurt.

Accordingly, Ned has since had some serious problems now surfacing along with aging physically. He took a lot of time off this past winter.

Lilly was terribly ill with a lung infection. Friends and relatives feared for her for several months.

Fidelity, which was handling almost one trillion dollars in America in 2000, is now down to under seven hundred billion dollars; a loss of over three hundred billion dollars in the fund market. In one year, business was down over one hundred billion dollars from a peak of around four hundred billion dollars in foreign lands.

The July 8th, 2002 issue of Business Week says otherwise stating the gross handle of the company is one trillion four hundred billion dollars. Let's do it in zeros: $1,000,000,000,000.00   plus $400,000,000,000.00 overseas.

That's one of the problems with private ownership. No one really knows, they tell you what they want to tell you and what they want you to know.

The stock market tables show poor performance for all large fund companies including Fidelity. The young fund managers have never dealt with a Bear Market. Many of the senior guys are retiring or quitting at Fidelity. Other companies are successfully stalking some of the better managers. The issue of Business Week mentioned prior says on the front page, "Here Comes Abby."

I thought there goes Fidelity.

CHAPTER 37 – IS THE PEN MIGHTIER THAN THE DOLLAR?

The trial was scheduled for mid-March, 2002. Preparation by both sides intensified as we neared that date. The case had taken a strange turn in my mind. Our side took a direction clearly aimed at proving Ned Johnson was a man of his word. An honorable guy you could trust with a handshake on any promise or statement.

Ned's group was out to convince the judge and jury that, though he may have made such promises, either he didn't mean it, or I should not have believed him. Therefore, it was my fault I did not get what I was promised. In other words, I had nothing in writing for six years and he could pay or not pay it, pay anything he wanted to, or keep or break any promise at anytime. That wasn't written either.

I had been in construction all my life, performing hundreds of million of dollars worth of work – some signed contracts, some handshakes, and some over the phone. I had never had anyone stick me, and I worked for some of the sharpest rascals in the construction business. The evidence of work done is powerful medicine in court, and any type of lien or litigation usually favored the working people. Ned told me to proceed. I did. Ned induced me to take action for his benefit; I did. "Promissory Estoppel," your promise induced me to take action, I did, and you pay. All of these did not work in Maine. The Judge and Jury was star struck. They wanted to show the trillionaire they were on his side against the poor bastard who was trying to take some money from such a great guy, a famous guy who they are honored to have grace their humble court. The judge had his wife and mother come to the trial.

I was standing in line at a Wal-Mart in Naples one day with three pads of paper and a bunch of pens. The fellow behind me said you must be going to write something big. I laughed and said I was.

"Are you a writer?" he asked.

"No, but I'm going to be."

"Good for you. What will be your subject?" he asked.

"It's about a lost friend."

"I know a little about the writing business. You have to have a unique subject or focal point."

"I've got one of the best."

"Good. Who or what is it about?"

"It's about a financial guy who you probably wouldn't recognize. Not many people do," said I.

"Try me, I'm in the business."

"It's about Ned Johnson of Fidelity."

He laughed, "I know Ned Johnson of Fidelity better than you can imagine."

"Oh yeah?"

Yes, I ran the trading desk for Merrill Lynch in Chicago for many years. We did billions of dollars with Fidelity over time.

I asked him, "When you made a deal to buy or sell with them, did you have eye contact, or a handshake, or anything in writing?"

"Are you kidding? It was all done with a phone call."

"Risky?" I asked.

"No way. We trusted Fidelity and they trusted us. Maybe we'd get a confirmation number on the phone, or a transition letter three or four days later in the mail. In our business if you weren't trustworthy you were dead. Fidelity has always had a good name. We had no problems."

I proceeded to convey my experience in as short a time as I could. He was incredulous.

He asked, "Are you telling me you are a good friend of Ned Johnson's?"

"Yes."

"And he made promises to you and didn't live up to them?"

I replied, "Yes."

"I find that hard to believe. If anyone in any business has a stamp on a company he owns more than Ned Johnson, I'd like to know who it is. So goes Ned Johnson, so goes Fidelity. What's the name of your book going to be?"

"Surviving Ned Johnson," I replied.

He started laughing and asked what will be the subtitle?"

"A Love Story, or Liar Liar Pants on Fire."

"Oh, Jesus, that is funny. Please remember me, I live in Naples. I want a copy of that book."

"Buy it at Barnes and Noble in about three months. I think it will sell to the financial world don't you?"

"Like hotcakes," he said.

"I don't think he'll like it."

"He won't, but the Vanguards and Schwab's of the world will eat it up. Good luck!"

The trial date approached. We were gearing up to do our best, but frankly, I thought it would be settled on or before we went through the courtroom doors, as did the reporters from the newspapers of the world. Several feeble offers amounted to nothing. At the deposition, Ned replied, when asked, if he felt he owed me anything. His answer was, "Nothing," followed by, "except the offer we've made regarding confidentiality."

When we sued Ned, we included Patty Hurley as a defendant because of her growing influence on him and consequently on his testimony.

Before the trial began, she was dropped as a defendant. Evidently, the lawyers considered her testimony not worthy of the court or jury – probably because of the language he had used in front of her regarding my heritage, my reputation, and me. I'm still puzzled by my lawyers agreeing to that move. Obviously he blasphemed me in his office (at Fidelity) where I had worked for five years, in Nahant (where I had lived for twenty-three years), to our mutual friends. (I was an asshole – he told them), and of course, on Mt. Desert Island, making sure none of the wealthy would hire me as a project manager. How in the world does an average guy fight back against these odds? Well the courtroom is one choice and since we didn't have anything in writing, why not put something down for the record. Again, lets hope the pen is mightier than the dollar.

I rented a room at the Sheraton Four Points at Bangor Airport. I wanted to be able to have my meals in a dining room for convenience and a homey atmosphere. It was the perfect choice with twin-oversized beds for anyone who came to the trial. My brother, Fred and his wife, Joan, came for the first day. My daughter, Nancy, came and stayed throughout, God love her.

The attendance in court was poor. Most of the reporters felt a settlement would be made before the beginning, but it didn't come. Nancy Garland of the Bangor Daily News was faithful to the process. After the trial I got a lot of calls from the media, the common thread stating how amazed they were Ned would stay four days to fight a risky, minor case not worthy of his attention.

I was amazed he went ahead with the thing. Certainly, money-wise, it was not sensible. It couldn't have meant anything to his reputation, which as far as promises and payments go, I believe he had lost that before in his own business.

CHAPTER 38 – WHAT'S YOUR NAME?

We entered the Bangor Federal Court on Monday March 4th 2002 at 8:30 a.m..

I was first on the stand. My attorney took me through the testimony, as did Ned's attorney. It was boring. There was nothing to add to what had already been written in the voluminous depositions from the year before. I will list the causes of action that survived to trial.

A request denied to us was his net worth, because they said it was not an issue. My net worth was and we gave it.

A request for his yearly income was denied, because it was not an issue. My yearly income was and it was given.

The charge of libel is, or was a serious charge, and was thrown out despite his ranting about me at Fidelity where I had worked. His term "he's an asshole" spread to our mutual friends in Nahant where we had lived for 23 years, and on Mt. Desert Island. I'm sure my services would never again be needed by the wealthy. Simply hiring the island workers all throughout the pretrial and trial cleverly silenced the tradesmen whom I worked with.

Breach of Maine's payment of wages statute was not applicable and thrown out. I agreed with this decision, since I was not on anyone's payroll.

Promissory Estoppel put simply is a promise the promissor (Johnson) makes that induces action by the promissee (me), which it did for ten months. He admitted the promise, but I lost because he didn't mean it and I shouldn't have believed him, says the judge.

Unjust enrichment is a clause that I conferred a benefit for Ned and family including Edward IV. I lost. Ignore the work and acquisitions I did. I should have done all this as any good friend would do. I wish to hell he would have talked to some other good friend (who could afford him) instead of me.

Imagine expecting a trillionaire to pay for work done. How the hell can he remain wealthy if he continued to pay his bills as promised.

The original sucker deal was one house, one year, one million expended, all my expenses paid for that year and 8% or $6,700.00 per month for the one year.

What did I do? Under his guidance, I built, bought, remodeled, including landscaping $11,200,000.00 of magnificent property, paid all my own expenses from December, 1997 up to August of 2000 and never received a penny from my labors after December, 1997.

All he concerned himself with was rent from the house I was supposed to have for the duration of the work, an obsession.

I'm lucky he didn't ask me for money for allowing me to work for him. Is something wrong with me? Is something wrong with him? Since the trial, he's lost over $300 billion in managed assets, dropped to the number three spot as far as size of companies in the same business. Not many of his funds are doing well. Big layoffs are coming in September of 2002. (Something has gone wrong with his horoscope. The stars are not lining up). A bunch of his star managers have fled to other companies including American Express. Fidelity has since canceled all business with AMEX, including credit cards "That ought to fix'em and everyone else that opposes me."

I have always believed in retribution. I've seen a lot of it in my fifty years of business. You take chances with your luck when you ignore the gods of fairness and reason. "Whom the Gods would destroy, they first make proud." His middle name should be "Hubris."

My lawyers worked hard for me. They believed in the case, the system, and most of all my reputation of fifty years, which research showed an impeccable record of truth and fairness to all my clients. They took the case for nothing since I had nothing to give. In the course of the work during the year and a half, I asked about their feelings. The answer was, "If we didn't believe in you and if we didn't think we could win we would not have taken the case."

If it is humanly possible for me to come back, I will see they are paid. Their answer to that was, they would not accept anything.

Those are the kind of people I like. This country needs that "Down Maine" sincerity. We need a whole lot of it across this spectrum of business cheating and lies.

At the trial, when it was time for him to testify he started giving the clerk his name, which was wrong. "State your name," said the clerk. "Edward C. Johnson," he replied.

Wrong. Why? He didn't want the jury of working people to hear his real name. It would sound like royalty, which is what he and a bunch of other Bostonians would like to be.

My attorney, John McCarthy spotted the ploy and said, "Just so there's no confusion with the other Edward Johnson's, you're Edward C. Johnson, III and your son is the IV?"

"That is correct," said E.C. Johnson, III.

Just for the record, Ned's father was Edward C. Johnson the II and his father was Samuel Johnson, who ran a clothing goods store somewhere in Boston, or nearby. That's where the connection with royalty began. That's what money does to plain people.

The rest of the testimony was full of instances of uncertainty at best and plain lies at worst. "My opinion," of course, or I should say, "I believe that is true," or "untrue," which is the way he answers most of his questions. If you say, "I believe" to the questions and someone shows that you're wrong, you can fall back on the fact that your belief was wrong, but you weren't lying.

When Attorney McCarthy asked a simple question about the cost of the shop/apartment being a little over two million, it took three full pages of questions and answers to get him to admit that the figure was correct and he knew it all along.

CHAPTER 39 – TRANSCRIPTS, "I BELIEVE"

Q: Now, has Dick Larson aided your family in either rebuilding or building or locating residences for members of your family?

A: He worked on the house in ... in Maine, and he also looked or brought ... called to my attention possible residences that might be bought by my son.

(No, I bought it.)

Q: That's Edward, IV?

A: That is Edward, IV, that is correct.

Q: Now, I think you indicated in your testimony that you participate in arrangements for the design and construction of the ... of your residences?

A: I ... do become involved in ... in some of the ... some of those arrangements, yes.

Q: And ... and I ... is it correct that you have an interest in Japanese ... Japanese-design concepts?

A: Well, I'm ... I'm interested in Japanese, Chinese. It's hard to distinguish.

Q: And ... and it's also correct that you've had the shop apartment complex that's been described in testimony in this case earlier built in ... at Long Pond in Maine?

A: That ... that is correct.

Q: And it had Japanese-design features?

A: It had Japanese-, Chinese-design features.

Q: Let me just take a second here. And did cost a little over $2 million to build the complete shop/apartment complex?

A: I don't know what the exact number is. I believe.

That's approximately the number.

(Baloney)

Q: I'm going to show you ...

MR. McCARTHY: May I approach the bench ...

THE COURT: You may.

MR. McCARTHY: ... the witness?

BY MR. McCARTHY:

Q: I'm going to show you what's been marked as Defendant Edward C. Johnson's answers to plaintiff's second set of interrogations.

A: Yes.

Q: And I refer your attention ... well, first of all, do you recall reading and signing these responses to interrogatories?

A: Yes, that's ... that's correct.

Q: All right. And let ... me refer you to page 5, which is the next-to-last page.

A: (Witness looking at document.)

Q: The page number should be at the bottom.

A: 5. Okay. That is a 5.

Q: And ...

A: It wasn't clear.

Q: And that's your signature at the end of the responses to the interrogatories?

A: Yes, it is.

Q: And ... below that, it indicates that ... that you ... that you appeared before a notary public and indicated the answers were true to the best of your knowledge, information and belief?

A: That is ... that is correct.

Q: All right. And let me draw your attention to the figure on page 3.

A: (Witness looking at document.)

Q: Do you see that, just below the middle of the page?

A: Which number was that?

Q: 16.

A: 16. Okay. Yes.

Q: Are you able to locate that?

A: Yes.

Q: And I'm going to read the question and answer to you.

A: Yes.

Q: It says, state the entire cost of the shop/apartment project, and your ...

A: Yes.

Q: ... and your answer was, the total amount paid for the construction of the shop/apartment project to date is approximately $2,015,000. And then in parens it says, this amount includes both capital and noncapital expenses, end of parens: is that correct?

A: I believe that is correct.

(He knows that's correct)

Q: All right. So I read the answer correctly, and the answer is correct, that it cost more than $2 million to build the shop/apartment?

A: That is correct.

Q: Do you know if that ... if that figure includes final landscaping costs?

A: I'm ... that's ... that's not clear to me.

(He knows it doesn't)

Q: All right. May I? Unless you want it ...

A: No, no.

Q: ... I'm going to take it from you. So it may be that it was more than $2,015,000.00?

A: I can't say.

(He can't tell the truth)

Q: But it was at least that amount?

A: I believe so.

(Here we go.)

Q: Well, I mean ...

A: It is so.

(Oh.)

Q: Okay. Thank you. Now, when the shop ... when the job was completed, did you ... did you begin to use the shop?

A: I've ... I've not used the ... the shop yet.

Q: And has the apartment been used?

A: It's been used, I think, just once or twice.

Q: All right. And it was ... was it completed and ready for use in June or July of 19 ... of 2001?

A: It was pretty close to ... pretty close to finished.

(It wasn't close.)

Q: So the actual project that was undertaken, the shop/apartment project, wasn't completed until at least June or July of 2001, and it might have been finally completed a little later than that?

A: I believe that is correct, yes.

(Here we go.)

CHAPTER 40 – THE TRIAL

I'm not going to bore you with the trial, but here's how you lose when the Judge hasn't got much time for the trial, and secondly, his mind is poisoned by the Johnson's attorney on a tax issue that had nothing to do with the case and was not supposed to be brought up! My tax issue wasn't presented to the jury, but was presented to the judge. It happened in 1988 and 1989 far away in Massachusetts. This is a classic case of human nature over judgment.

We ended up with five legal issues. The issue of libel was not allowed, nor was several others by the Judge before trial.

I lost according to the jury because I had nothing in writing.

Promissory Estoppel went to the Judge and was returned three weeks later. The Judge said no.

Unjust Enrichment went to the Judge and three weeks later, no dice. I want to focus on the Judge. The jury wanted to go home and work, and pay their weekly bills. They were bored listening to lawyers arguing for two old guys, one rich and one poor.

The Judge's two counts were important to my team, and me because they were obvious. There were no questions or answers that could deny I was asked to do the work, because it was done. I did it because for some strange reason the project manager who was assigned couldn't get the project going. This I thought had to be obvious and I was pleased the Judge was going to handle the two counts.

Unfortunately the Judge was cut-off at the pass. He was handled, instead, by a clever defense attorney who knew more about human nature then he does about ethics, or the law. I don't blame him, nor do I think my lawyers failed. They too were cut-off by this clever guy.

In 1988, the Bank of New England went bankrupt for 14 billion dollars. Many people who owed me money went down with the bank. I almost went bankrupt, but because of my and my wife's assets, we sold everything and paid the bank and all the payrolls, except some withholding. Our creditors declined to sue us. In fact, many creditors called and thanked me for 38 years of great business and wished me good luck.

I had paid all the taxes I could for the corporation, but owed the withholding for about $500,000.00 representing several months of payroll. Every time I put remaining checks into the corporate accounts, the IRS took it, so I quit. I worked for Fidelity for five years, meeting with the IRS on occasion. I was concerned they would attach my pay. They said no, because of my age and the fact my wife was a non-working dependent.

We went to Maine in 1995 to work for Ned and opened a small corporation under complete ownership of my wife. She would administer the corporation and do all bookkeeping to earn her salary of $11,500.00 per year, and I, as an employee, got the same. We consulted with our CPA in Boston and our lawyer in Maine. What we did was every bit as legitimate to avoid my tax problem as Fidelity's offices in Bermuda to avoid taxes on overseas business.

What does all of that have to do with the Maine construction and the broken promises? "Limine" means certain subjects are agreed ahead of time, not to be brought up in court. It's Latin for eliminate. I thought my tax problem was not going to be presented in court, nor was Ned's mental health as presented to me over the years from 1989 to present.

My taxes were not discussed with the jury, but were brought up with the Judge in a side bar meeting recorded, thank goodness, by the typist.

Johnson's Attorney convinced the Judge I was a tax cheat and a liar, and he wanted to impeach me as such. The judge wouldn't allow it, but I'm sure it stuck in his mind after the public trial and affected his decisions three weeks later.

The Judge would not allow the Jury to see or hear about this long ago problem of taxes, but Johnson's attorney didn't care about the jury. He was working on the Judge. He was painting me as a tax cheat and liar in the Judge's mind, and was successful beyond his wildest dreams.

The tax issue was and is a red herring. We did all the law allows to protect my wife's last assets and had the necessary records to prove this in all courts.

The non-issue, however, became an issue in the Judge's mind and he decided I had done nothing to earn any money. The building built itself for eleven months through the winter somehow, and he had protected Mr. Johnson from the clutches of a liar and a cheat. Hero's come in the form of all kinds of settings. Johnson was not enriched at all, though I spent millions on the buildings.

What I detected from Ned's testimony and those witnesses who were called was what might be called evasive blandness.

Mike Frasier, the supervisor for Bond Builders, had been the on-site superintendent for the big house. We were good friends. During the construction of the shop, I used to kid with him and the carpenters. If they complained mildly I would reply. "Hey, don't complain, at least you're getting paid. I'm working for nothing." I said this to other trades in a joking manner. I never dreamt what was meant to be funny would come true when Mike took the stand and said I had told him I was working for nothing.

On the stand, Mike had to answer the question "Did he ever tell you he was working for nothing?" Mike had to answer truthfully and he did. I just wished he had added "jokingly."

Dick "Tater" Gray testified he enjoyed working for me, for Ned and for my replacement. Well why not? He, like all the others, had been given a substantial amount of work during the court proceedings. I don't blame anyone for not wanting to lose the Johnson account.

Brian Reading, the architect on the shop, testified to the quality of the team we had assembled. He loved the building considering it to be his best and my best through a successful collaboration. The apartment on the second floor may be the finest piece of design and construction ever achieved on Mt. Desert Island. I left before the lower floors were finished in rubber tile and neon lighting. How sad.

Joe Tracy, mentioned earlier as a great designer of furniture and works of art, including the Chinese ceilings, testified as did the others. The pleasure of doing the project and the atmosphere I created prompted everyone to do their best for Ned – that was my goal.

The ex-president of Crosby Advisors, Dick Walsh, when asked if he had ever seen Fidelity or Ned, or for that matter Crosby Advisers give out a percentage of cost contract said, "Absolutely not. Never, never did I ever see anything like that from anyone associated with Ned. Why, that would be insane." I think that was damaging testimony against us and our claim of verbal agreements.

Unfortunately, for us, he was flat out wrong and we didn't pick up on it. In fact, in the five years of construction, we never heard or saw, or received one piece of paper from Dick Walsh himself, or anything that even resembled a contract, and very little if any paperwork from Patty Hurley. I couldn't tell you to this day what their letterhead looked like. We should have rebutted his statements at that moment. The architect, McHenry Associates contracted with Ned for the main house long before I got there. When I arrived in July of 1995, I called Bill, as Ned instructed, to get him started again. We met and eventually that first day I asked about his contract agreement. "It's eleven percent of the cost of construction," said Bill.

"Oh?"

"Yes, eleven percent of one million dollars, which is the budget."

"What happens if we go over?" I asked.

Bill looked blankly at me and said, "I don't know."

"Do you have that in writing?"

"Yes."

Ned gave a go-ahead to hire landscape architect Karen Kettlety for thousands of dollars at God knows what percent before I was brought back to do the shop. There was nothing in writing. When her bills became impossible, he asked me to fire her, which I did.

Bill McHenry had a non-written verbal agreement on the shop, also Blanchard and Gray had been told to do all blasting and excavation with no-contract, only verbal assurance.

Joe Tracy – no contract – verbal. Why waste time. The only contracts given for $11,000,000.00 worth of work came from me to Bond Builders, which proved to be useless in the face of 600 owner-mandated change orders, and that includes Edward the Fourth's house and mine at Prays Meadow.

Did we track and check all these changes? Yes, certainly using a change order log system that works well with the billing system recommended by the A.I.A.

Neither Walsh, Hurley, nor Ned ever processed one piece of paper to my knowledge on the work in

Maine. Dick Walsh never came to Maine. Patty Hurley came once or twice, both over five and one-half years. Yet, they were experts on all of it. In fact, Walsh came as an expert witness on something he'd never seen or knew anything about. His testimony on contracts was so brief and boring it was not recognized by my lawyers or me as the most significant part of the case and we blew it. Ned's group, without knowing it, had taken a hell of a chance bringing Walsh up from Boston and had gotten away with it. Ned and Patty, who gave input to their attorney, knew so little about Maine that they didn't know that Walsh didn't know what he should have known. We were only slightly dumber. I let it go by with a yawn. A costly mistake for me and all of my team. It had to be that way dealing with unsophisticated, but talented people and an eccentric billionaire. We had to push in all directions to get the work done, or it would have cost us double. We'd still be there. Maybe that's what he wanted. He didn't want to finish. Keeping us on a string by making us believe we were needed for the future kept the job young in his mind. Money didn't mean a thing to him throughout the process until someone convinced him I was a bad guy wearing a black hat. With Ned, I had noticed you could change his mind as the job was concluding simply by blowing in his ear.

Not wanting to leave Bill's verbal percentage contract up in the air, I did re-negotiate it ending up with 11% of $1,000,000.00 and 8% of everything over that. Four million more was spent so the renegotiation saved Ned 3% of $4,000,000.00, which was $120,000.00. Never known to this day or acknowledged. I made many legitimate deals in five years that saved Ned more than all he should have paid me and made their requests for rent ludicrous.

Losing the court case was a hurtful loss of money, self-esteem, and reputation, but some losses are acceptable and we put up with those mentioned as acceptable, losing a close friend is not. It's no good, it bothers you mentally and physically, it just hurts too much. When the elderly in the family pass on, it's usually acceptable – maybe death is an easing of the pain of life. Losing one child, or a young boyhood friend, or any friend is not acceptable ever and remains with you throughout life.

As you age, you have fewer friends and your circle shrinks through loss by death, or tragic circumstances out of your control, including loss of friendships. All loss is tragic and responsible through separation issues, for more mental illness, I believe, more than anything else. When Lilly predicted he'd drive me crazy, she hit the nail on the head. I think I've gone nuts.

CHAPTER 41 – LOSING FRIENDS

The end of the trial, the fine friendship we had established dissolved, all the fine qualities of loyalty, unspoken love, admiration and trust found in such a link-up between two guys becoming curmudgeons of the first water was over. We had treated ourselves to openness, gruffness, self-to-self cursing, such as Mark Twain characters in Huckleberry Finn. He couldn't hurt my feelings, nor, I thought, could I hurt his. We blasted away, sometimes to other peoples' surprise at the treatment we gave each other, but they didn't know, nor understand that type of affection between men. We were equals because money wasn't a factor in our relationship until Ned decided it was. The Penobscot ritual of blood brother was a serious ceremony although treated lightly at the time and reminded me of the death of my friend "Dickie Quinlan in 1938."

When you watch something fine die, a friend, or friendship, whether you're eight years old or seventy-two you step back astounded. You wonder what will help and what action can be taken to mitigate the horror you've just witnessed.

My family lived in a small section of Peabody Massachusetts in a little cottage in Lake Shore Park. Bounded on one side by Brown's Pond and the other by some fine woods featuring a large outcrop of rock ledge called "Baldly Rock."

There was one road in and one road out. We were isolated from the real world of traffic, trucks, buses, and noise – a tight knit community. In the summer of 1938, three events occurred that helped shape my mind, three events, which influenced me for the rest of my life.

The towns north of Boston on the North Shore were dealing with a polio epidemic. Parents worried about the air, the moist air of August as a carrier. Rumors swept the communities about lettuce, tomatoes, or fruit bought at the local markets. The kids were told not to swim in Brown's Pond. We had to be in the house after supper when the streetlights went on.

Then we were hit. Mary Hutchins from two streets over was in the Peabody Hospital with a suspected case of Polio. Her father John Hutchins spent days at the hospital. At night when John walked up our street, Glendale Avenue, I was rocking inside the screened-in porch with my parents and sister Mildred. Usually he came by late in the evening, the warm dusk of night, a lonely figure under the streetlights. My father would put his paper down, open the screen door and walk out to him and in sympathetic muffled tones ask about Mary.

When he came back in, he was serious as he explained her condition for that day. It was never good news. Nobody knew what to do. This went on for several evenings until the night he went out, talked to John, and then shook his hand. He came back to announce Mary Hutchins was dead at eleven years old.

"Mary Hutchins can't swim in the lake, or hide and seek a wooden stake. For she can't move nor can she talk, she lies beneath a sacred rock." A children's rhyme for the end of summer, soon stopped by the neighbors and our parents.

The boys of the neighborhood spent hours up running and playing in the woods. There were numerous trails, which were known only to us. We knew our way to the various exotic stops. There was the fox den, the ledges, the lemon squeeze, the stone quarry, the bat cave, and finally, the climb up the steep face of old "Baldy Rock." There was a break in the face, about six by six, that you could tuck into and hide. The climb from that point was steep and dangerous. Of course, we all did it. When a new kid was with us, he had to do it too as a form of initiation.

When you made the climb, you were at the top of the rock, a huge area of grass, stones, and one very tall "high tension wire tower." It tied in with other towers a half mile away in each direction. The heavy strands of wire looped gracefully down the steep face of Baldy and on to the east tower on the shore of Brown's Pond. We visualized as kids riding that half-mile down slope of cable with some kind of invented wheel; what a ride that would be.

One warm afternoon late in the day and late in the summer, a bunch of nine year olds, including me, had completed the loop hike and arrived on top of old Baldy. Four boys, two or three years older then us, were lying on the grassy sections looking directly up at the blue sky with low white cumulus clouds drifting by towards the ocean, which was east by ten miles.

This was a fun thing to do because all you could see was sky. You felt you could drift straight up or imagine you were already there. Sea gulls drifted by heading towards the Atlantic. Looking north the sky scene was pierced by this tall-boxed steel tower, which appeared on semi-cloudy days as if it might fall down. Of course, it was cloud motion that caused the illusion. The tower was latticed starting wide at the base and narrowed as it topped out at eighty feet. At the top, the steel out rigging held the porcelain shock proof cylinders at six or eight feet on both sides, from a distance it looked like the letter "F" in Chinese.

Latticing on four sides began ten feet above ground as a safety margin, after that, the steel resembled a ladder and could be used by the lineman to climb to the top for repairs and additions. On occasion, one kid standing on another kid's shoulders would grasp the top rung and climb several nearby rungs up to maybe 20 feet.

Twelve of us lay on the grass enjoying the illusions and pointing out to the group what the clouds resembled in each ones imagination. If the crowd agreed with the comment, you'd feel like you'd scored a point. Looking back 64 years, I recall the conversation among the four older boys when it took a dangerous turn. Red Scanlon, a tall freckled kid spoke, "I wonder who's climbed highest on that tower?"

Nobody responded, they didn't know.

"Do you think anybody has ever reached the top?" asked Red.

"Yeah, the lineman," one kid said.

We all laughed.

"I mean Park kids," said Red.

"It can't be done," someone said.

"I can do it," said Dickie Quinlan.

"You can't do it," said Red who was also Quinlan's cousin.

"I'll bet you five bucks I can touch the top," says Quinlan.

"You're on," says Red.

By this time, we had all sat up and looked at two kids who were proposing to tempt fate. I was concerned as were the rest because it held a danger that was unnecessary, foolish and we just didn't need that.

One of our gang said he was leaving, joined shortly by several others. This type of thing made us feel we were breaking the law, getting into trouble, the police would see Dickie high on the steel, climb up old Baldy and arrest all of us. My father wouldn't stand for that. Besides giving me a good whack on the bottom, he'd be ashamed of his son being arrested.

Two of Dickie's friends, including Red Scanlon, boosted him up to the first steel bar. Dickie was a strong, wiry, agile boy and hoisted himself on top of the angle iron. He sat there swinging back and forth with complete confidence. I had started part way down the ledge face, but stopped in fascination with two other kids and stared, mesmerized I guess. I couldn't leave. I had to see the act of daring.

Dickie started up, leaping lightly to the next rung. This was dangerous and would be until he had gone far enough up to be able to reach without jumping. At forty feet the rungs got closer and his progress accelerated as he climbed. He had half the climb left when Red worrying about his five bucks yelled.

"Don't forget you have to touch the top." Dickie continued up past the first strands of wire on the lower end of the outriggers, climbed past the center sections of wire, reached the top wires three feet below the joined narrow steel, took one more rung, reached for the goal and touched the top. Suddenly, a pale blue flame enveloped his whole body outlining Dickie perfectly against a darkening sky. He stiffened, let go of the steel, threw both arms over his head as if cheering himself for winning, then slowly he left the steel rung and began to fall, arms and legs perfectly motionless. His back horizontal to the ground he drifted away from the tower like an Olympic diver.

He landed. All of us froze. We couldn't comprehend this occurrence. We waited for Dickie to move. He didn't. Red and the other two on the top broke the trance and ran to help Dickie get up or something. Red leaned over his cousin and he put his face near Dickie, then looked up, yelled down to us, and said, "He's alive. He's gonna be okay. Run down and ring in the fire alarm at the corner." We took off down the ledge to the talus slump, then ran for ten minutes down the steep decline, raced for the red pull box on Glendale Avenue, broke the glass with the small ball peen hammer and pulled and pulled. We were soaked. We had run through a small stream that was bridged further down at Lajoie's house. We knew the fire engines would come to the Fairview Avenue entrance, the park access nearest the firehouse on the main street near the elementary school. One kid stayed at Lajoies bridge, while I and the other kid ran to meet the engine and guide them to the remote area.

The engine came blasting around the curve, stopped, picked us up and we guided them to what they thought was a fire. The engine was so noisy we couldn't tell them what had happened until we reached Lajoies. We jumped off and the leader asked, "What is the problem?"

I answered, "A kid fell off the tower."

"How far did he fall?"

"From the top."

"Jesus Christ," he grabbed the truck phone and called for police and ambulance service. He grabbed my arm, "Is he dead?"

"I don't know. I didn't look."

He said to me, "Stay right here."

They unloaded blankets, two stretchers, and several metal cans of drinking water.

"How the hell are we going to get up there?" the leader asked his men.

I said, "There's a steel cable around the side of the ledge older people use when climbing."

"Good, take us there right now," then turned and said to the men. "You won't need boots, let's go." By this time, neighbors had gathered as had the darkening afternoon. The firefighters followed me around the steep ledges to the old cable rail holding on with one hand and their equipment with the other. They began what proved to be a tough climb.

Sixty-four years later, I still vividly remember every detail and in my mind, the time frames did not work in Dickie's favor. We took at least thirty minutes to reach the top and cross the rocky plateau. Two boys were standing on the edge of rock moss. Red was sitting holding his cousin's hand. Dickie's clothing was partially burned off except for his rubber sneakers. The firemen took over and gave Dickie some water. They tried to sit him up a little. He had a deep reddish tinge to his face and peeling chest and arms. He said nothing nor made any sound, but he was alive.

The leader of the fire crew said, "Well boys, I think it's time for you fellows to leave. We'll bring him down and you can see him later. Get started now please."

Red said, "I'm not leaving. He's my cousin and I'm not going down without him."

"Does he live near you?"

"Yes, next door."

"I want you to go down son. You need to tell your mother or father, and they will tell his family he's been hurt. Can you help me by doing that important job?"

Red paused, but understood the leader's request and I guess it made sense because he started running. I was asked to leave and was thanked by the leader with the mumbled approval of the entire group. I looked back when I reached the edge, because I was going back the way the kids did, down the rock face. It was a surreal scene, a young wounded boy and five sad firefighters in fire helmets and rubber capes standing looking down at a tragedy. I left.

By the time I reached the stream, there were police cars and ambulances with their red lights flashing. I walked down to Lajoies Bridge. A crowd had gathered. My sister was there. When she saw me she started running home to tell my mother I was all right. They both came back later to wait with the crowd to see Dickie Quinlan. My mother beckoned me to stand with her. I refused with a wave.

With the help of the police and the ambulance attendants, they got Dickie down the mountain and started toward the bridge. There were earthen banks above both sides of the crossing. I had stationed myself on top of the right hand side as they clumped across with grim looks carrying the stretcher. Dickie turned his head slightly and looked at me through dazed eyes, no emotion, but seeming recognition. He was badly burnt on all exposed surfaces, which had peeled. What we couldn't see was the damage done by the high current to the inside of his body or the damage from the fall.

I never saw him again. He died seven days later at Peabody Hospital. I never forgot Dickie. I never forgot, nor have I to this day, that at seventy-two I lost a friend, who at eleven years old lived and died in one lifetime in one day in a late August summer, and the next day life went on, different for some. We had all aged overnight...the earth moved faster for us and we didn't know it, but we felt it.

In late September, they had a memorial service at the Samuel Brown School scheduled for 3:00 p.m. While we marched by class to the auditorium, I slipped out and started for home. I was alone. I cut through the woods to the pond; the wind had whipped the water to froth against the gravel shore. I walked in it deeper and deeper until I was in up to my knees. I went home and my mother scolded me for getting my school pants and shoes wet. I went upstairs, laid down and slept until my father got home.

I woke when he called up the stairwell, "Are you coming down?"

"Yes."

I went down to eat expecting to be chastised, but nobody said anything. That night I had a fever, but in the morning, I was okay and went to school. My father came home at the end of the day with a new bike I had asked for from Sears. I didn't have one. It was blue, white, and beautiful. It was a twenty-six inch and cost twenty-eight dollars, including a front light.

CHAPTER 42 – START CARING

I'm talking to my agent. She takes an adversarial approach to the book to show me why the book may not sell too well.

"Dick, if the book is all about you, forget it."

"It isn't," I replied.

"Well, who or what is the subject? What's the hook you have? You have to have one to induce the public to buy."

"It's about Ned Johnson."

"Who the hell is Ned Johnson?"

"He's the private owner of the world's largest mutual fund call Fidelity Investments or Fidelity Management Research," I replied.

"Well," she said, "I've heard of Fidelity of course, I thought Peter Lynch owned it."

"No, Peter Lynch ran the Magellan Fund from 1972 until 1995. Now he's a board member."

"Okay, okay, but what the hell do I, or anyone else care about Johnson as long as he makes money for me and his clients?"

"You *must care* and *know* because, as I said before, he *owns* the company personally. No corporate outside board, no listing on any stock or bond exchange, in other words, no checks and balances by anyone probably including any Federal Agency, despite what you hear. Does he conform to the SEC rules? Let's hope so.

Vanguard and Schwab are listed on the exchanges, which require full disclosure of performance. Fidelity is not. They disclose what they want to.

Vanguard has 15,000,000 clients, Schwab has 12,000,000 clients, and Fidelity has 17,000,000, give or take on all three totaling 44,000,000. Let's say that five percent are professional investor observers who make their living investing. That's who wants to know everything there is to know about Johnson. That's 2,200,000 potential buyers. Let's say only half buy. That's 1,100,000. I'll settle for that and you and the rest who don't care can continue to earn your living your own way and hope Ned makes money for you, and your lottery ticket pays off."

"I'm not trying to insult you in any way. You are, like me that average investor. We are the majority, but the minority adds up. Actually, Ned doesn't care what the market does. He has plenty of his own cash. He makes money on people like us when we buy or sell. He gets us going up and coming down. He's got a better deal than the lawyers."

City of London Telecom was a major success for Ned. This guy thinks big. He opens up three companies in three different countries, probably with some of your money. You see, you don't know. Metro Red opens in Argentina. The economy of that country heads for the drain shortly thereafter, so Metro Red files for bankruptcy without a second thought. That leaves its creditors in hock and Red heads off to the sweet guitar sounds of "Sayonara."

If you are observant and know how ruthless he can be, you might want to double-check what plan he has for your money. You might decide to sell C.O.L.T., which is probably where the money came from to start in South America.

In a book entitled, *Fidelity World* by Diane Henrique, a New York Times business writer, the author says you can learn about the history of the company, but nothing much about the owner. This book is the closest biography about Ned ever written and it's unauthorized, not a press agent's bland presentation censored by anyone connected to the great Oracle. In my opinion, you must care and know, or all we stand for will be lost. It will be all about money and things.

There may be some mistakes or even lies in this book, but if so they were told to me by Ned Johnson. I believed what he told me. We all read about some of the wealthy guys like Warren Buffet, with his down-home appearance, his forays to the local Dairy Queen for lunch and a small sundae. Just a regular guy, huh? Or, Bill Gates, who has taken up bridge with Warren as a sometimes partner, cute team – benefactors of charitable giving for the needy. Well, Warren just may be the smartest man in the country and tough as nails on a deal. He's a bottom fisher for bargains, sometimes a shark, sometimes a flounder. He collects from everyone, the rich, and the poor. He keeps ten and gives back one; the old Robin Hood game for the sake of a good image.

Gates likes to play bridge, but he's an expert at Monopoly. In fact, he not only beats his competition, he beats the country. Read some of the business news and listen to the bleatings of his competitors as they try to break a 95% monopoly. He is a dangerous guy. The press softens his image by reporting other people run Microsoft now. Bill has semi-retired to his forty million dollar home, occasionally coming out.

At least we know something about Buffet and Gates, but not many know anything about Ned. He, like his company, is just as compassionate as a computer. I believe he is convinced of his infallibility, which has led him to become a control freak gone wild

I admire the American businessman as the best in the world. Remember a few years ago, Japan was being touted as, "taking over the business world." My brother, Fred, was working for General Electric traveling worldwide on jet engine sales when this period of American business bashing was taking place. He'd make me a martini and one for himself, and begin a friendly tirade on foreign countries.

"Dick, I've dealt with many foreign countries. They're not as good as we are. Some are particularly overrated. They're being held together by incestuous relationships within the country."

I said, "I think you're right, but the system seems to work."

"Nope," he says, "You can't borrow your way to profits."

I believe Fred is typical of the training he got at General Electric. Starting at seventeen in the apprentice program, he became part of mid-level management, for which GE is now famous.

The lessons he learned from GE revolved around the theme, "Do the right thing," "Be honest with yourself and your clients," "Arrogance leads to failure every time," and last, "Try to make deals where you and your client come out well and everyone's happy."

You know, I think that is right. Being mean-spirited, always having someone else to blame, dishonesty towards workers and friends – that's no way to be or to live. That's not the Ned Johnson I thought I knew in 1990. That's not the guy who told me I was responsible for everything in Maine in 1995, and who let me down in 2000.

Near the end, upon learning, one of his best friends and admirers, Sarah Larson, had had a mild heart attack, he responded to my face, "That's your problem." Is that where he is now?

It's taken two years to get over the loss of Ned's friendship. Never mind the promise breaking and meanness. Loss of friends and relatives are devastating to the mind. My childhood friend, Dick Quinlan's life was so short and ended so tragically. I carried the sadness all my life.

The loss of Ned Johnson's friendship, like the loss of my childhood friend Dickie Quinlan is a wound that will never completely heal

THE END

If I had it to do over, if I could turn back the clock and save this fine friendship would I do it? No. It would only have gotten worse had I caved in to Ned and Crosby Advisors. I would have become one of them and there are enough of them around already.

I'm a poor guy now. Not much in assets, but my wife knows and knew when we married in 1951 she had someone who would stand up for her and our family in a fearless manner. We never accepted lies as truth just to get along, nor did we go along for the same reason.

In our old age together, we have absolute love and respect for each other. We laugh at ourselves, our exploits through the years, handling all crises, giving honest opinions, and, as Sarah often says to our friends, "We are a bit unique in that we went from rags to riches and back again in one generation."

And, you know what? We handled the ragged, the in-between, and the rich in the same manner.

"And that has made all the difference."[1]

---

[1] *The Road Not Taken*, Author Robert Frost

For more information about Dick Larson Books:

Email us at:

dlarsonbooks@aol.com

Or write:

Dick Larson Books
PO Box 11629
Naples, FL 34101